a kind of dedication

Words written in blue
to be read after take-off
by a first-time flier
who suffers from vertigo:

at last
here's what it's like
(though you may not want to know)
you're winging it
flying
the real word
on top of the world
a time-capsule
                    nowhere

AIR

EDITED BY PETER CARVER

PETER MARTIN ASSOCIATES LIMITED

Introduction

Air is one of four collections of Canadian writing which make up the **Elements** reading series. Other titles are *Earth*, *Fire* and *Water*.

Taking off from our particular earth, breathing clean air, feeling the wind through forests or across the fields, this is the stuff of renewal for Canadians. These are experiences we thrive on. To fly, glide, parachute, sail, leap is to escape urban clutter, and routine. If we can't fly literally, we can at least launch out into other levels of release, speculate on what haunts us, fall in or out of love, sing, dance, enjoy nonsense and fun in our special way.

The desire for flight and float is the theme of *Air*. Prose and poetry, song and story, all the selections relect the many-faceted life of this country registering at once our diversity and our shared feelings and insights.

Here is mythology we can share. War aces Billy Bishop, Bill Barker—and Roy Brown from Carleton Place, Ontario, the pilot who finally downed the famous Red Baron. A lament for the last of the Beothuks, the Indian race extinguished by the white man in Newfoundland. Tall tales from the lumber camps of the Gatineau hills.

Here are personal moments of exhilaration—"highs". The lift in spirits that comes to a melancholy father with the surge of a kite in Hugh Hood's "Flying a Red Kite". The shock felt by the broadcaster who has forgotten to prepare mentally for his first parachute jump in "Mati Laansoo Tests the Law of Gravity".

Here are Marconi, CB freaks, TV—electronic air.

Here is music.

Here is the wind.

Air is lightness, humour, whimsy. Mishaps for Max Ferguson on live television. Sly digs at the post office by singer Bob Bossin. Barbara Frum's recording of an unbelievable political speech. W. P. Kinsella's funny, poignant account of a meeting between white bureaucrats and an Indian family. Pied Pumkin's tongue-in-cheek entry in the Olympic song contest.

Our material is drawn from all regions of Canada, by familiar and unknown writers. It's a feature of our culture that for each name with a national reputation, a dozen no less eloquent authors languish unrecognized.

The bland Canadian stereotype simply doesn't stand up against the richness of anecdote, adventure and colour present here. It's a richness expressed in strong language, the reflection of vivid experience.

Peter Carver

Contents

I, Icarus

There was a time when I could fly. I swear it.
Perhaps, if I think for a moment, I can even tell you the year.
My room was on the ground floor at the rear of the house.
My bed faced a window.
Night after night I lay on my bed and willed myself to fly.
It was hard work, I can tell you.
Sometimes I lay perfectly still for an hour before I felt my body rising from the bed.
I rose slowly, slowly until I floated three or four feet above the floor.
Then, with a kind of swimming motion, I propelled myself toward the window.

Outside, I rose higher and higher, above the pasture fence, above the clothesline,
   above the dark, haunted trees beyond the pasture.
And, all the time, I heard the music of flutes.
It seemed the wind made this music.
And sometimes there were voices singing.

Alden Nowlan

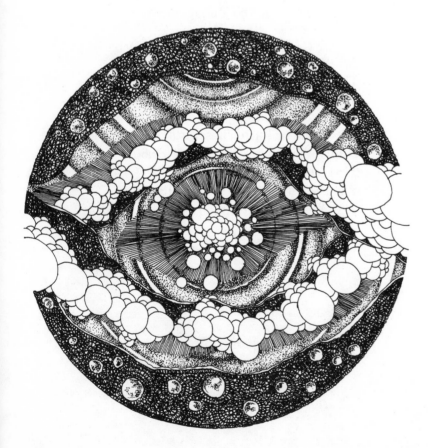

6

Mati Laansoo Tests the Law of Gravity

Last year I tested the law of gravity for the listeners of "This Country in the Morning" by jumping off an airplane. People who heard the program might remember me talking about skydiving with instructors and parachutists—when I asked the students what they felt before and after their jumps, they said: "scared" and "terrific" respectively. And I'm sure listeners remember my terrified voice before and during the parachute descent.

The actual descent lasted less than three minutes. It took another three hours to edit the tapes for the radio show, and I must admit that I spent six long and difficult days trying to write it down on paper. But I didn't waste all that energy and effort merely to describe a few seconds, during which I encountered the most terrifying moment of my life. My purpose in writing this is to communicate something else—something rather interesting that I discovered, something that didn't come across on tape.

It was mid-October 1973 and I was in Vancouver when I agreed to make the jump. I had to take a parachute course first, and I had to take it in a hurry—even in Vancouver, the weather is getting tricky for a parachutist by October. There were other complications. My worst problem was how to get the jump on tape: I couldn't just strap my fifteen-pound Uher tape recorder on my chest, and even a cassette recorder would be too bulky. What I needed was an efficient transmitter and receiver, small yet powerful enough so that the receiver could pick up my signal from the air. When I managed to borrow one such unit from CBC television news in Vancouver, I discovered that the transmitter would stop whenever I turned my back to the receiver, connected to my tape recorder on the ground. If the equipment failed to pick up my voice during the jump, I'd have to repeat the performance.

So on that fateful day, I spent all my time fiddling with wires and antennae and cursing at the prospect of wasting all this effort. Even during the final briefing before boarding the plane (wearing a crash helmet, shod in paratrooper boots, clad in a jumpsuit, with a parachute harnessed to the back and a smaller one secured to the chest), while everyone was repeating their instructions, my mind was elsewhere. And that's why I was still desperately tugging at the microphone taped to my neck as we stumbled awkwardly from the clubhouse towards a tiny four-seater Cessna 180, idling noisily at the edge of a soggy pasture.

In order to make room for everyone, the interior of the plane had been stripped of everything except one seat, on which crouched a bored guy with a crewcut and thick bifocals named Jack, who was to be our pilot. Under the instrument panel, with his back crammed into an unbelievably tight niche, I discovered Jerry, our jump master. Jack proceeded to warn us to lean well forward, or the overloaded plane would fly straight into the high-tension wires above the end of the three hundred-yard-long field of mud. This statement scared the hell out of everyone, so we obediently bent over on our knees, with our heads pressed between our rumps and laps. There was a loud surge of noise and a terrible pounding sensation as the little plane bounced over boulders and across ruts; the straining engine performed a minor miracle, and we were airborne.

The noise was deafening; everything vibrated or rattled. After what seemed like hours, from my cramped position I could see Jerry yelling at me. I could see him yelling because his mouth was moving and the veins on his neck were bulging. He motioned to me that we were over the "drop zone," and that I was to jump first. My eyes followed his finger pointed at the target area, a tiny dot 3500 feet below us, where I must land. Suddenly there was a blast of cold air mixed with the roar of the engine as the upward-hinged hatch whipped open.

I won't bother the reader with my trivial thoughts as the pit suddenly yawned at my feet, as the sting of adrenalin filled my body. I will only describe precisely what I did next.

Carefully, I placed the boot of my left leg on to a twelve-inch pipe sticking out from the fuselage, and cautiously clamped my left hand around the diagonal wing strut. As I groped to clamp my right hand along the upper length of the strut, the wind force was so unexpectedly powerful that my right leg swung out behind me and the helmet banged against the wing above my head. And there I perched—frozen with fear—suspended in the slipstream, with the loose fabric of the jumpsuit flapping wildly around my legs.

At that moment, it flashed across my mind that, with all the worry and fiddling with the transmitter on the ground, I had omitted one crucial detail: I had failed to prepare myself mentally for the actual ordeal coming up. At that moment I also happened to remember from my

game is my demise.

The static-line has been cut! Somebody has replaced the chute on my harness with a backpack and, as I fall, a canopy does not appear above me because the backpack ejects a variety of cups and plates and thermal underwear! Too late, I see Jerry laughing hysterically and checking off another name from the list on his clipboard. My god, he's holding up a Jeroboam of champagne with the other hand! He's going to drink a toast with the pilot, who's wiping tears of mirth from his eyes. . . . You idiot, how could you be sucked into this madness?

But Jerry slaps my leg again, harder this time, and then this madness dissolves because I figure, what the hell. And all of a sudden, I am absolutely nowhere. In the distance I can hear someone screaming: "Arch thousand . . . two thousand . . . three . . . " (it's me doing the yelling, you see), and then all kinds of incoherent words are coming out of my mouth.

Then, ever so lightly (as the harness tightens around my thighs and shoulders), my fear turns to grateful relief and I descend into the perpendicular. A huge red-and-white-striped canopy billows overhead and the blue curvature of the Pacific Ocean sparkles ahead of me. The white-capped Coast Range looms to my left and the checkered quilt of miniature farms and fields is spread out below me. There is no sensation of movement. I hear a gentle whisper of wind through the shrouds. Soon the ground becomes larger. Reaching up for the steering toggles, I find them quite responsive. I can see the target (a fifty-foot circular mound of pea-gravel) which has grown to the size of a dime already. I make out the fluorescent orange of the drop master's coat, directing me. And I steer accordingly, letting the wind drift me nearer. Slowly turning, over the clubhouse—the ground is rushing up very quickly now—I'm going to hit a barking dog, staring up at me stupidly. And then: thump! I land on both feet and remain standing as the canopy drops over me—and it's all over.

Some excited people who have been around the tape recorder rush up to tell me that they heard me loud and clear. The drop master offers his congratulations. I landed only a hundred feet off target, and I'm grinning from ear to ear because everything had worked!

There was no cry of triumph, just some knowing looks from a few experienced skydivers. The sort of looks you get after an indescribable experience—only to be shared among the select

high-school physics that, should you be unfortunate enough to fall without the benefit of a functioning parachute, you will accelerate at an increasing rate of 120 feet per second/per second, until you attain a speed in excess of 120 miles an hour. You will also soon come to an abrupt stop—but only after bouncing a few hundred feet into the air, after the first impact with the turf.

So when Jerry slaps me against the leg and yells, "Go!"—I can't *move*. I'm stuck to that silly little pipe with one foot, holding on for dear life and staring wide-eyed at this madman whose obvious few, as it were.

The last person I saw as I drove away into the sunset was an instructor lying on his stomach on top of a bench, demonstrating the position of arms and legs during free-fall. It occurred to me while I was negotiating the ruts on that same muddy field where a few hours earlier I had been bumping along in the other direction, that a lot of people would go on from here to real skydiving. This is falling free in a controlled spiral, and holding hands with other skydivers for a timeless moment like some strange ritual. Some people will repeat this performance thousands of times, and I know why they do it.

But just as I came to a stop to look for traffic, before driving up on to the paved road, I happened to look up into the sky. And way up above, I saw the little plane carrying another load of parachutists. I knew exactly what was happening inside. I could visualize the bored expression on Jack's face as he guided the frail craft upward through wide circles to the proper altitude. I could see his hairy arm reaching across the crowded cabin for the hatch handle. In fact, if I'd looked long enough, I'd eventually have made out a tiny little black dot for an instant before actually hearing the sharp crack of the canopy opening; then, the stationary circle of a little striped parachute, while the plane flew away. And as I pointed the nose of my old Chevy pick-up homeward, I got the picture that somehow, that first experience can never be duplicated.

It's like the song I heard on the car radio as I tore away down the highway. It was Alan Price, from his album *O Lucky Man*, and I turned the volume way up loud to hear the words. He was singing:

There's no easy days
No easy ways
Just go out there and do it!
And smile while you're making it . . .
Laugh while you're taking it . . .
Even though you're faking it . . .
'Cause nobody's gonna know . . .

from *Peter Gzowski's Book About This Country in the Morning*

Canadians are the greatest nay-sayers in the world. A good motto for Canada would be, "It will never fly, Orville."
—Mavor Moore

Rescue Flight

October 1932

The message clicking in to the Army Signal Corps post on the outskirts of Edmonton was halting and so garbled that it was almost unintelligible, but it told a story of anguish and despair.

The two Sens brothers were in desperate need of rescue. Returning to their wilderness hut from a routine patrol, they had tried to light their stove, fed from a nearby natural-gas pocket. The leaking stove blew up in their faces.

Both of the brothers were seared blind. Their faces, hands, arms and chests were severely burned in the flaming explosion. But, using his elbow on the telegraph key, Joe Sens was able to hammer out an agonized plea for help.

In the meantime, a neighbouring trapper, alerted by the roar of the explosion, had arrived at the cabin. He could do little to relieve the suffering of the blast victims, but under their gasped directions, he was able to rig a telephone on to the telegraph line and converse with the Signals authorities in Edmonton to explain their predicament.

Unless they got medical treatment soon they could not hope to survive. They would face a slow and painful death in their remote cabin, 150 miles north of Edmonton in the bleak Canadian wilderness.

Rescue appeared hopeless. There were no roads in that wilderness, and no flat areas where a plane could land. Normally, the local rivers and lakes provided natural runways for the planes that were their only link with civilization. In summer the planes landed on the water on pontoons, in winter on the ice on skis. Between seasons, when the forming or melting ice was not strong enough to support a landing, nothing flew in that area.

It was between seasons now.

In Edmonton Major Jim Burwash, C.O. of Army Signals, himself a weathered veteran of the northern telegraph patrol on which the Sens brothers served, paced the brown linoleum of his small office.

"Those two boys are going to die and there's damn-all we can do about it! Any pilot trying to land on the river or lake ice would crack up and go straight to the bottom. But get one of those bush pilots out here right away. At least we can talk about it."

Half an hour later the warped storm door of the shack was yanked open, and along with a gust of cold air and a flurry of snow, a tall broad-shouldered young man clumped into the room. Major Burwash had asked for a bush pilot; he had got Grant McConachie, the youngest and wildest of them all.

While McConachie shook the snow from his rumpled brown hair and his windbreaker, Burwash quickly told him the story. McConachie immediately picked up the phone to Pelican Rapids and confirmed with the trapper that despite the cold snap there would be no hope for an ice landing on the Pelican River or on any of the lakes in the region. And the solid timber all around made a landing on the ground apparently out of the question.

But McConachie tried another tack. The nearest lake? Ten miles from the Sens cabin along his trap-line trail. He had a small shelter on the shore. Yes, the water would be low at this time of year. There was a fairly level strip of beach. Couldn't say for sure, but there might be just enough spread between the tree line and the water for a small plane to get down.

"I'm going to try a landing on that beach," McConachie shouted to the trapper over the makeshift phone line. "You take the boys over to Oboe Lake at first light tomorrow morning. When you get there, be sure to light a fire so the smoke will give me the wind direction for landing."

He outlined his plan of action to Major Burwash. The blue Fokker he had been flying on the barnstorming circuit all summer was still on wheels in the Edmonton hangar. He could take off before dawn with a doctor, a mechanic and medical supplies. They might have to pancake on to the beach and probably would damage the plane, but he was sure that nobody would be injured.

The doctor could look after the blast victims. Then they would just have to wait till the lake froze over solidly enough for a plane on skis to come in and pick them up.

The grizzled Signals veteran squinted dubiously at young McConachie. "It's a wild scheme. Mebbe just crazy enough to work," he said, "But I can't be responsible for taking a chance with a doctor. If you and your mechanic are prepared to make the try on your own, you've got my blessing. You can fly in with the medical supplies, and the doctor can give you full instructions. You'll just have to do your best."

As he negotiated the snow-covered dirt road from his home in Calder to the Edmonton airport in the 5 a.m. darkness of the following morning, the young pilot's mind was on the Fokker's most serious shortcoming as a wheel-plane . . . no brakes.

Instead of brakes the Fokker was supplied with a hook attached to the tail which was supposed to plough into the ground and halt the plane. In theory, and on soft landing strips, it was fine; on the frozen lake beach it would ski along uselessly.

Landing on a narrow strip of shoreline less than a thousand feet long without brakes—well, even he had to admit that there was an element of sheer madness in this mercy flight.

Another fact nagged at the big twenty-three-year-old's confidence as he thought about the rescue venture. He knew that as a plane loses flying speed on landing the force of the slip stream diminishes, making the rudder ineffective. For steering, the pilot has to use a touch of brake on either wheel. No brakes, no steering. Not a cheering prospect with the spread between the lake and the trees only slightly more than the Fokker's wingspan. The slightest misjudgement would send him careening against the trees or into the lake.

As he pulled up on the grass ramp at the airport McConachie was happy to note a light in his corner of the hangar, which meant that Chris "Limey" Green was already at work on his checkout of the engine and airframe.

Limey was a bush pilot's best form of insurance, a skilled and dedicated mechanic. McConachie had filled him in about the flight the night before. Green was aware he would be riding blind in the enclosed cabin during a perilous landing, but his only remark had been a question, "What time do you want the ruddy beast ready to go?"

In the murk of the empty airfield McConachie lowered himself into the open cockpit of the Fokker, switched on the twin magnetos and prodded the starter. The Jacobs belched loudly, then roared to life. He went through the familiar drill. Flex rudder, elevator and aileron controls, flick a finger against each instrument on the panel . . . altimeter, fuel level, engine revolutions, oil temperature, cylinder head temperature . . . As the engine warmed in the crisp air he pulled a helmet over unruly brown hair, buckled the chin strap and watched the oil temperature needle move slowly from red to green.

Then he lowered the heavily-padded goggles. He advanced the throttle, tested both mags at full power, eased back on the revs, waved the chocks away and jockeyed the aircraft over the uneven surface of the cow pasture that served as Edmonton's airport.

As the Fokker slanted upwards into the early morning sky the young pilot exulted once again in the thrill of release from the bonds of earth. But now the familiar exhilaration of flight was spiced with the anticipation of a challenging adventure. Climbing steadily on a northerly compass heading, he watched the ground recede gradually into a featureless haze far below. Soon the first slanting rays of the sun were glinting on the lacquered fabric of the Fokker's wing. At least the weather would not be a problem this day.

At altitude, the continuous thunder of the engine exhaust stacks directly ahead of his windscreen diminished perceptibly as McConachie throttled the Jacobs back to cruising power. He adjusted the elevator trim for level flight, fanned a practised glance across the altimeter, airspeed and tachometer readings on his instrument panel, then relaxed at the controls.

As the blue Fokker droned northwards McConachie found himself reflecting on the intimate relationship that soon evolved between a pilot and his aircraft. The Fokker responded to his slightest pressure on the controls more like a living thing than a mere assembly of fabric and metal.

During the long year past, most of his waking hours had been spent in the cramped and solitary world of this cockpit. Now he felt as if he were almost an integral component of the blue Fokker. He could anticipate every quirk and whim of its airborne behaviour, could sense its predictable response to each swell and current of the restless air ocean in which it swam.

McConachie was aware that he possessed a native aptitude for flying, so he had no doubt of his ability to pull off at least a survival landing in the wilderness. He recognized that his arrival might well prove to be what the wits would call an "organized crash." The Fokker might take a knocking about. But he and Limey would come out of it intact. And so, he prayed, would the wooden carton lashed to the centre of the cabin floor. He was acutely conscious of its contents: carefully padded bottles of tannic acid, assorted quantities of special ointments, bundles of antiseptic gauze, rolls of bandages, and the doctor's typed instructions for the treatment of burns. He winced as his thoughts turned to the victims waiting at Oboe Lake.

High over the white spume of the still-unfrozen cataract he identified on his map as Pelican Rapids, McConachie eased the control column to the left and applied a touch of rudder, banking into a steep turn on to a westerly heading. Minutes later he sighted his destination and throttled back, sloping the Fokker into a steep gliding descent, to circle at low altitude and size up the situation.

He remembered the subsequent events well:

"It was by now a bright sunny morning and there was no problem of visibility. It was a big lake covered with thin ice. I could see the trapper's cabin and three men on the shore.

"The shore line, which appeared to be clear of obstructions, was frozen marsh overgrown with bulrushes, and there was a narrow margin of sand, just enough for one wheel, between the overgrowth and the lake ice. I figured if I could set one wheel down along that sand margin, the other on the flat shore ice, there was just enough room for the wing tip to clear the trees. Nothing to spare, though.

"The trapper had followed my instructions and had a fire going so the smoke would give me the wind direction, but he got a little overenthusiastic and there was so much smoke that it blinded me completely as I flew in low over the beach on the landing approach.

"After two attempts I had to give up that idea and decided that instead of landing into the wind, which is normal so the head-wind will give you the slowest possible ground speed, I would have to try a landing down-wind. This, of course, stacked the odds higher against me because the wind would be pushing me along faster instead of acting as an air brake.

"However, there was no choice, so I had to rely on my experience with this particular aircraft to bring it in at the lowest possible airspeed. It was like treading an invisible tightrope. Just a shade slower and I knew the plane would stall and drop from the sky out of control. I kept the nose high, with a lot of power on, so we were actually wallowing down through the air in a power stall, practically hanging on the propeller. Then, just as the wheels were rattling over the first of the bulrushes on the shore, I chopped back the throttle completely. I cut the ignition switches to minimize the danger of fire if we cracked up, and pulled the control column full back to complete the stall and uttered a small prayer.

"It was pretty rough as we plopped down into those bulrushes. I thought the first impact would drive the undercart right up through the floor. Then we bounced and jolted along the beach. There was a frightful moment when I thought we would keep on going right through the trapper's cabin. Without brakes, and with the tail-skid hook dragging uselessly on the rock-hard surface, there was nothing I could do to slow the landing run. Luckily, we rolled right up to the door of the cabin

and came to a stop almost beside the bug-eyed trapper and his two patients.

"It was quite a shock to see those poor fellows at the cabin. You couldn't even recognize them as human beings. They had been burned so badly they had great white water-blisters hanging down from their faces right down to their chests. There were angry red welts covering their hands and spreading right up their arms. Their faces were so badly seared and swollen they couldn't see. They weren't actually blind but their eyes were swollen tight shut. Their noses were almost burned right off. It was a terrible thing to see."

It was clear that if McConachie waited for the ice to freeze, the Sens brothers would be dead. They would have to make the return flight at once.

While McConachie applied first aid, Limey inspected the aircraft. The Fokker had not escaped undamaged—in fact, its fabric underbelly was split from end to end. Apparently, it had caught the stake of a muskrat trap as they landed. Limey sewed it up in hopes that it would hold together for the return flight. McConachie then gave his attention to the problem of taking off from the short strip of beach. As he put it, "With no brakes on the Fokker there was nothing to hold the aircraft while I could rev up the engine to full power before starting the run down the short strip of beach. The strip was so short that it seemed certain I would run out of runway before I could get off the ground.

"We hauled the aircraft back as far as we could up a slight slope and tied the tail to a tree, running the rope over a stump we could use as a chopping block. I told the trapper to stand by with his axe while I ran up the engine to full power, then to chop the rope when I waved my hand.

"Meantime, Chris had loaded the heavily bandaged patients into the cabin and made them as secure and as comfortable as he could.

"We were taking off into the wind, and I figured that with the down-slope and starting with full power we had a good chance of making it. I pushed the throttle wide open, waited for the engine to pick up full revs, then gave the signal. The trapper swung his axe, the rope parted and away we went rumbling through the bulrushes.

"With the full power from the start, the blast of the slip stream over the rudder gave me full control, so it was not too difficult to thread the needle of the narrow beach between the trees and the lake. We didn't seem to hit any obstructions, but suddenly, just before the wheels left the ground, there was the most terrible vibration. I thought it would shake the plane to pieces.

"I throttled back as much as I dared but by this time there was no other choice. We had to either take off or crash, so I manoeuvred the Fokker out over the lake, just skimming over the tree-tops, figuring it was better to crash through the ice than into the trees if we had to go in.

"The shuddering continued. It increased when I put on more power, diminishing as I pulled the throttle back, but I couldn't figure out what it was. The engine seemed to be working all right. Chris couldn't find any damage to the fuselage. However, we were able to gain some altitude and continue the flight."

It was a long trip home with the plane trying to shake itself apart all the way. But, finally, McConachie shut off the engine for a dead-stick landing on the Edmonton airport where police cars, ambulances and doctors were waiting.

As the injured men were whisked off in ambulances, McConachie clambered wearily down from the cockpit and was surrounded by reporters and photographers. Meanwhile, Limey studied the propeller. Shocked, he called Grant over to see it. It had split right down the middle as it chopped through the heavy bushes on the take-off. The only thing that had saved it from flinging apart was the metal binding. They had flown all the way home on a thin strip of metal!

The story has a happy ending. After four or five months the Sens brothers recovered and returned to their solitary cabin at Pelican Rapids. They owed their lives to the "wild scheme" thought up and pulled off by the brashest young bush pilot of them all, a man destined to become one of the most colourful and controversial figures in the world of aviation—Grant McConachie.

from *Bush Pilot with a Briefcase*, by Ronald A. Keith

Incredible Achievement!! Canadian War Ace Downs Five Enemy Planes!!!

William Barker's victory tally now totalled forty-seven, which placed him fourth in the roster of Canadian aces, with fellow Canadian Billy Bishop's seventy-two victories unequalled by any other living flyer. That was the standing on the morning of October 27, 1918, when Bill Barker packed his personal belongings and prepared to return to England. He had been staying with No. 201 Squadron, a Camel unit with a large number of Canadians in it, when orders had come through for him to return.

Higher authorities now felt that he had had plenty of time to acquire the first-hand information necessary to teach young pilots the tricks of air fighting. Barker's life was now considered too valuable to risk in the daily dogfights over the western front. The order had been final, and Barker realized that this time there was no chance of arguing his way out of it. So with his baggage packed and ready for ground transport to England, he walked to his plane, carrying only a small kit bag for the return flight across the Channel. Mechanics had been busy that morning stripping the Snipe of its war loading in preparation for the more peaceful life of a training station. Though the guns were loaded, the Aldis peep sight had been removed and only the open ring sight left in place.

Barker climbed into the cockpit and waved away the mechanics. The plane roared down the field; then it seemed to head off in the wrong direction. An hour later, phones jangled in the squadron's operations office and breathless front line artillery observers related to the thunderstruck aviators of 201 Squadron the garbled details of one of the most astounding air battles in aviation history.

Barker had indeed flown in the wrong direction. He had purposely set his course for the battlefront. Later he admitted that he wanted "one last look," and possibly one last tangle with German fighters before calling it quits.

After take-off he held the nose of the Snipe in a steady climb, the little aircraft responding beautifully to his touch on the controls. At 15,000 feet, he levelled off and flew parallel to the front lines. The town of Cambrai was behind him when he swung the plane into a half turn and held his course steady into German-dominated air space. Climbing again, he brought the labouring Snipe up to 19,000 feet. This was almost the ceiling for the plane, and Barker found himself breathing quickly in the thin air. Then, far ahead, he spotted puffs of smoke from bursting anti-aircraft shells high in the sky over the Allied section of the front line. That spelled out a warning: enemy aircraft. Barker dipped one wing and banked away towards the anti-aircraft fire. Black crosses glinted in the sunlight and Barker made out the silhouette of a high-flying German observation plane. German two-seaters of 1918 were particularly efficient in the thin air of extreme altitudes, and there were few British machines that could catch them. Nevertheless, the Snipe, with part of its war loading stripped away, responded when Barker again eased the stick back, and rose above its ceiling of 20,000 feet.

Reports vary about the type of aircraft Barker was stalking, but it was probably either a late model Rumpler or the formidable Hanoveranner, an armour-plated machine that was among the best fighter aircraft. Both these aircraft were deadly foes. The Rumpler, described as one of the finest two-seaters of the war, could reach 21,000 feet and carried three machine guns. An earlier model of the Rumpler was credited with shooting down the famous French ace, Georges Guynemer.

Besides their own defensive armament, two-seaters on reconnaissance missions rarely travelled alone. There were invariably a number of "little friends" hovering in the sun, ready to pounce on

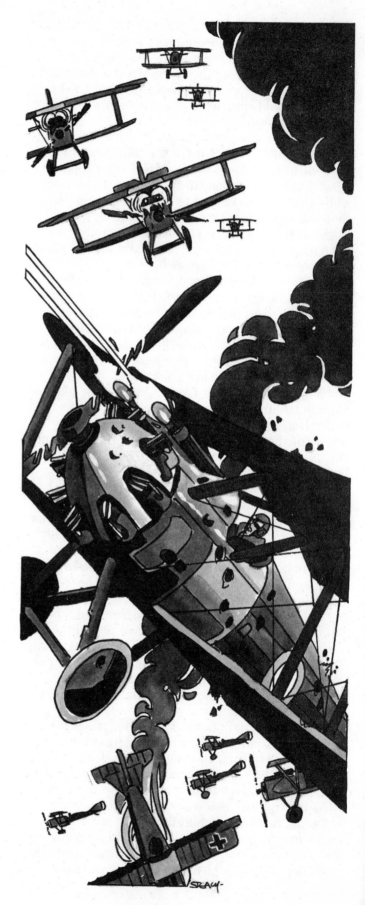

14

any Allied plane that came too close. Barker was fully aware of his danger as he nursed his labouring plane into a position for attack. He searched the sky for signs of enemy fighters, but found none. By this time he was on a level with the two-seater and the enemy pilot had evidently spotted him, for the German plane turned eastward towards home. Barker dipped the nose of his plane slightly to gain flying speed and the chase was on. The two planes were now heading at top speed directly into German-held territory. The risk to Barker increased with every mile, for at any moment a German formation could come between him and his own lines, cutting off his chance of retreat.

The German plane was flying straight and level in a bid to outrun the faster Snipe. Despite the fact that his controls were now mushy owing to the height, Barker sacrificed some of his speed to gain a few more precious feet of altitude, then lunged at the two-seater. The German manoeuvred violently to give the gunner a clear field of fire, turning first to the left, then to the right. Barker nosed down until he was below the enemy's tail, then pulled his Snipe into a gentle climb, hoping to reach the blind spot beneath the tail where he could rake the other ship with his fire without danger.

But this German proved to be wily. While the pilot yawed the plane violently, the observer swung his gun over the side and bullets thudded into Barker's plane. It was a point-blank shot at the slowly climbing Snipe and every bullet struck home with telling effect. Barker pulled away from the damaging fire and circled the two-seater warily. His plan of attack had been foiled by the Germans' expert handling of their equipment. He realized then that his only course was to try and out-shoot the observer. Again he approached from the rear, but this time at an angle, hoping to make a deflection shot which would knock out the enemy plane before the observer's fire could be brought to bear on him. Again bullets beat a tattoo against the thin fabric of the Snipe, but Barker grimly held his course. At forty yards, the enemy plane was centred in his ring sight and he thumbed the firing button on his control stick. A stream of Vickers bullets stitched a line of holes across the fuselage of the two-seater. Barker watched as his enemy plunged towards the earth far below, a greasy plume of smoke marking its fall. It was victory number forty-eight for the Canadian. Groggy from the lack of oxygen and the excitement of the fight, he felt a mild surprise as parachutes blossomed

behind the burning aircraft; it was the first time that Barker had seen parachutes used by a plane crew.

There was no time to marvel at the new development. A vicious blow struck him in the right thigh, and bullets hammered his instrument panel to junk. In sudden panic he looked behind him—straight into the winking muzzles of two Spandau machine guns. A German fighter had arrived too late to help the two-seater and was now out for vengeance. The bullet which struck Barker was an explosive round, and it had shattered his leg. Almost fainting with pain, he lost control of the Snipe, which fell off into a flat spin. The enemy fighter followed him down, evidently satisfied that the British plane or its pilot was disabled. After a 2,000-foot plunge, Barker managed to regain control, and, pulling the stick back to his safety-belt, he turned to face his attacker. With his first burst he torched the enemy plane.

This was not the end, though. Faint from pain, Barker had set his course for the British lines when tracers again whispered past his cockpit. He looked above him: the sky was filled with black-crossed airplanes. His plane had passed right through a formation of at least twenty of the lethal new Fokker D-7's. It was sheer instinct that guided Barker's hand as he pulled the stick back, at the same time tramping hard with his good leg on the rudder bar. The Snipe spun around and Barker bored in towards the closest Fokker, his guns hammering. His glazed eyes, peering through the ring sight, soon told him that he was actually attacking two planes, one right behind the other. With a ferocity born of desperation, Barker continued his charge and was rewarded by seeing both Fokkers, their wings riddled with bullets, fall off into power spins. Meanwhile a third German fighter loomed in his sights. At ten yards Barker's bullets struck home and the German plane exploded.

Then Barker was hit again; this time the bullet broke the bone in his left leg. The world turned grey, then black, as he lost consciousness. Again the Snipe fell off into a spin. The rush of air revived him and instinctively he levelled off right in the centre of another German formation.

The bullet-torn Snipe had fallen below 15,000 feet now and the beleaguered Canadian fell back on the one manoeuvre that could save him. He put the Snipe into a tight turn and as he circled he fired at everything that crossed his path. With a German right behind him, he tacked himself on the tail of another brightly coloured Fokker, watching with dazed satisfaction as his bullets went home and a trickle of flame, followed by a fiery gust of smoke, burst from the Fokker's motor. Again he felt the shock of a bullet and his left arm went limp—an explosive bullet had broken his elbow. Once more he fainted and his plane fell into a spin. His pursuer drew off, certain that he had finally downed this apparently indestructible Canadian.

However, at 12,000 feet the higher oxygen content of the air revived Barker, and once more he pulled up his battered plane just in time. But the nightmare continued: Barker found himself in the midst of a third echelon of German planes. Contemporaries believe that Barker must have tangled with an entire flying circus stepped up in flights, or *Jagdstaffeln* (hunting squadrons), of twenty planes each. As he lost altitude in his uncontrolled spins his plane passed successively from one flight to another. Ground observers later swore they counted as many as sixty planes lining up in "taxi rank" for a shot at this madman who did not know when he was beaten. Barker said later he was certain that he was doomed and had resolved to sell his life as dearly as possible.

Now, in the midst of the lowest level of the German circus, the severely wounded Canadian aimed his plane at the nearest Fokker. Barker wanted to ram this German before he died. He poured bullets at the German plane as he roared towards it, and watched in dazed disbelief as it disintegrated in mid-air, so that he literally flew right through the wreckage of the enemy plane.

Again the infuriated Germans closed in and Barker's plane shuddered under a fresh onslaught of bullets. Tracers tore into the gas tank of the Snipe, but luck was still with him, for his plane did not catch fire. Switching to his auxiliary tank, he kept the tattered Snipe in the air by sheer force of will. No man's land was skimming beneath his wheels; ahead lay the British trenches and safety. Barker fought back the black tide of unconsciousness and, with his remaining strength, hauled the control stick back into his stomach. The Snipe lifted slightly, soaring over the tangles of barbed wire that marked the British front line, then settled wearily to earth. The wheels snubbed into a shell hole and the plane nosed over.

Scottish troops who pulled Barker's unconscious body from the wreckage had watched most of the fight from their trenches. They had seen Barker's suicidal lunge at the last Fokker and his intention had been obvious. They were astounded to find the badly shot-up airman still alive.

Barker was in a coma for two weeks and only his

amazing vitality saved his life. His wounds left him with permanent and painful disabilities. When he regained consciousness, he learned that the war was over and he had won the Victoria Cross—the third Canadian flyer to receive the Empire's highest award in the First World War. Barker's epic battle remains a classic in the annals of aerial warfare. It brought him promotion from the rank of major to lieutenant-colonel. He was given credit for the destruction of five German aircraft in the battle, which brought his final tally up to fifty-two aircraft and nine balloons destroyed, the sixth highest total in the entire RAF.

The true measure of Barker's courage is illustrated by his attitude to life after the war. The wounds he had received refused to heal properly and he was in constant torment. Yet walking only with the help of canes, he continued to lead the active life of a flyer. He helped to found the Royal Canadian Air Force and, with the great Billy Bishop, started Canada's first airline. There are no medals for this kind of courage. Barker's refusal to surrender to his crippling injuries reveals his unconquerable spirit more than all his deeds in battle. Ironically, in March, 1930, while making a routine test flight of a new plane at Uplands Airport, Ottawa, the man who had survived the most one-sided fight in aviation history crashed to his death.

from *Canada's Fighting Pilots*, by Edmund Cosgrove

Billy Bishop— Solo Air Duellist

Billy Bishop was yet to have his most memorable day, however. It all started just before dawn on June 2, 1917. The flying field was still in darkness when Bishop rose from his bed, pulled his clothing on over his pyjamas, and left his quarters. After a brief stop at the mess hall for a gulp of scalding tea and some army biscuits, he whistled for his dog Nig and walked to the nearby hangars. Inside the hangar Bishop's mechanic, Corporal Walter Bourne, was fussing over the engine of the Canadian's sleek, blue-nosed Nieuport. "All right, Corporal, roll her out."

Seated in the cockpit, Bishop pulled an oil-stained leather helmet over his tousled, light brown hair, at the same time making a last minute cockpit check. Then he nodded his head and the mechanic swung the prop. The engine wheezed, then burst into life as gas flooded the cylinders. At Bishop's wave, the mechanics pulled the chocks from under the wheels. Corporal Bourne's shouted "Good luck, sir!" was lost in the roar of the motor as the plane lunged through the open door of the hangar and swung off the field into the darkness, heading for the grey eastern horizon.

Hedgehopping to avoid anti-aircraft fire, Bishop headed deep into German territory. Fifteen miles behind the German front line, an airfield was receiving the first telephone alarm that a single British fighter had crossed the line at dawn and was heading their way. Officers shouted orders and sweating mechanics wheeled seven fighters from their hangars and swung the props to warm the engines.

It was too late. Over the trees that bordered the field, Bishop's plane burst on the scene like a hawk on a chicken coop. At an altitude of less than one hundred feet, he swooped down on the line of fighters, his Lewis gun stitching the wings and motors of the grounded planes. One Albatros began to roll forward in a take-off and Bishop pointed one wing at the ground and spun around after it. His gun stuttered sparingly and fifteen bullets thudded into the cockpit and engine of the taxiing plane, just as it lifted from the field. It dug in one wing and ground-looped itself into a pile of wreckage.

A second plane had started down the field and Bishop pulled his control stick back into his stomach, achieving altitude for a second attack. He roared after the moving plane and this time it took thirty bullets. The enemy machine piled into the trees at the end of the runway. Then numbers began to tell. While Bishop was occupied with the first two, another pair of Albatroses scooted down the field and soared into the air, banking left and right to avoid him. Climbing fast as he reloaded his Lewis gun, Bishop closed with the nearest, which had reached an altitude of 1,000 feet. Under the whip-lash of Bishop's gun, pieces came away from the German plane, and it crashed less than three hundred yards from where it had taken off.

By this time ground fire and bullets from the fighters had turned Bishop's plane into a tattered wreck, but he lunged after the fourth Albatros and emptied a full drum of ammunition into it. As the plane tumbled wildly to escape the bullets, Bishop, noting other enemy planes taking off from the field, decided to call it a day. Reaction to the intense excitement set in, and on the flight home he had to fight dizziness and nausea. Four enemy planes chased him all the way to the lines, but he managed to outfly them and bring his heavily damaged plane to a safe landing at his own field. He was greeted by a crowd of excited airmen; they had learned of the fight from observers in the British balloon line who had seen the whole affair from their swaying baskets. When Bishop was asked how many machines he had shot down, he replied with unconscious modesty: "Only three. One got away."

Later investigation revealed that he had severely damaged a number of other planes on the ground and had wounded the pilot of the fourth German fighter which had "got away." Bishop's report of the mission against the enemy aerodrome was carefully scrutinized and substantiated before, on August 11, 1917, he was informed by the Commander of the air contingents in France that he had been awarded the Victoria Cross—the first Canadian airman to receive the decoration. Bishop quietly thanked his superiors and left the squadron office.

Fellow pilots, curious as to why he had been summoned, received no satisfaction from Bishop, who walked back to the fight line where Bourne was working on his plane. After a moment of

conversation about the repairs, Bishop added, almost as an afterthought: "We've won the Victoria Cross."

New squadrons were now being given a little more time to familiarize themselves with terrain and tactics before going directly into action. Bishop used his experience as a flight instructor to skirt the regulation which kept him on the ground. He managed to obtain permission to lead his new men in daily practice formation flights, teaching them the value of tight aerial discipline and showing them how to use their eyes. Though airmen were required to have perfect eyesight, Bishop, the lone wolf of the past, knew only too well how easy it was to fail to see an enemy fighter lurking under a cloudbank or riding high in the sun, shielded by the blinding rays.

Each day he would lead his entire squadron over the lines, and later, back at the air base, would question each man carefully about what he had seen. "Didn't see a thing, sir," said one new man. Bishop promptly gave a detailed account of the types and position of almost a dozen German planes that had passed their formation during the flight. With lessons like these, he hoped to give these young flyers a chance of survival.

However, while conducting these instruction patrols which stressed the value of working as a team, Bishop still carried out his solo patrol work. Often, after leading his squadron safely back to their own lines, he would drop out of formation and vanish. He knew that the time for lessons was

growing short. The squadron would soon be thrown into the fighting, and he would be forced to return to his desk.

Bishop was sent back to England to receive the medal along with the Distinguished Service Order and the Military Cross which had been awarded him for earlier exploits. His record now showed forty-seven confirmed victories. As one of the senior RFC aces still alive, he was now too valuable to be risked in the daily rough and tumble of air fighting. Besides the loss of his experience if he were killed, another consideration was the crashing blow to civilian morale that would inevitably follow. Britain had recently suffered the loss of Albert Ball, who had been killed in action. The Secretary of State for Air, Winston Churchill, was not going to allow the death of another hero to spread a pall of gloom over England. So despite Bishop's vigorous protests, he was ordered to leave the front and go home to Canada on leave.

After completing his leave and returning to England, Bishop found himself posted to a training command. Like Barker, Bishop rebelled, but in a more restrained manner. By the spring of 1918, his repeated pleas for a return to active duty were heard and he was sent to France to command a new squadron, No. 85, equipped with the fast, heavily armed SE-5 fighters. Since squadron commanders were forbidden to fly, Bishop's job was to "fly a desk," sending other men into battle while he remained on the ground. It was a task quite alien to his personality, but orders were orders.

It was during this period that Billy Bishop established his reputation as one of the greatest solo duellists of the war. In twelve days he shot down a total of twenty-five enemy aircraft, a record that few, if any, combat pilots ever equalled. By comparison, it took the leading American ace, Eddie Rickenbaker, almost a year to score an equal number of victories. On his last day of front line flying, with orders in his pocket to leave at once to join the staff of the Air Ministry in London, Bishop made his final solo offensive patrol behind the German lines and shot down five enemy aircraft.

After the war, Bishop was sent back to Canada to help organize the Canadian Air Force. Then he left the service and tried his hand at business, but he missed flying and did not remain too long in any particular field. He proved to be an able writer, and his books on aerial warfare are considered models of their kind. At one time there was a suggestion that a documentary motion picture about his life be made, but unfortunately it never got beyond the planning stage.

When the Second World War began Bishop again offered his services. His dream was to be given command of a fighter wing. Again he was considered too valuable to risk, and again it was Winston Churchill who refused his request for active duty. Churchill gently reminded him of a similar plea he had made in 1918 and told him truthfully that he would be of more value to the war effort in recruiting the young men needed to man the air fleets of the Second World War. Reluctantly, Air Marshal William A. Bishop, VC, DSO, MC, agreed with the great statesman.

from *Canada's Fighting Pilots*, by Edmund Cosgrove

The airplane is an invention of the devil and will never play any part in such serious business as the defence of a nation.

Hon. Sam Hughes,
Minister of Militia
and Defence for Canada, 1914.

The End of the Red Baron

Then, of course, there was the end of Richtofen. The great German ace, conqueror of eighty British machines, and chief organizer of the large German formations which opposed the unceasing air offensive of the RFC, was finally killed, in April, 1918, by a bullet believed to have been fired by Captain Roy Brown, of Carleton Place, Ontario. Richtofen had aroused the admiration of friend and foe alike. He never showed any remorse or distaste for the killing of an enemy—he had the professional soldier's attitude to the grim task—but he had always treated the pilots who were taken prisoner with the strictest courtesy. He had fought with the greatest British airmen, with Bishop, with Collishaw, with Ball, with Hawker (whom he killed in combat) and they all spoke highly of his skill.

Richtofen's end came on a day when a young relative was being introduced to air fighting. Richtofen was keeping an eye on the new pilot, to steer him safely through his first fight. On the same day a young Canadian pilot, later to become famous as Wop May, the pioneer bush pilot, was also experiencing his first combat. May was successful in getting on the tail of Richtofen's protégé, which brought the old master down in a screaming dive to protect his kinsman. May was about to become Richtofen's eighty-first victim, when Captain Roy

Brown saw his danger, and flew to his assistance. He fired a burst at Richtofen from the right-hand side, and a single bullet struck the great German pilot, penetrating his heart, and killing him instantly.

The red triplane was seen to crash behind the British lines, and Brown reported the victory, without having any idea who the enemy was. Late in the afternoon word came through that the Red Knight of Germany was dead. Two Australian machine-gun crews on the ground had fired at Richtofen, and they claimed to have shot him down, but a very careful examination proved that the bullet must have come from the air. The seat of Richtofen's triplane was brought to Canada, and is still a treasured relic in the Royal Canadian Military Institute in Toronto.

Though the British flying men were pleased to have eliminated this dangerous enemy, nevertheless they were generous in their tributes to him. "If only we could have taken him alive" was the common sentiment expressed about a skilful and courageous pilot.

from *Knights of the Air*, by John Norman Harris

Flying/Spring of '44

He had twelve days leave when I met him in Montreal
We courted a week then got married
He wore his uniform
I wore my grey silk suit and a hat with a veil
My mother shook her head and said
You hardly know the boy

But it was the spring of '44
It was such a crazy time
And he seemed so brave
So full of glory
With his talk of planes and the sky
I remember him saying—

"Oh flying
Well the Hurricane is a damn fine plane
And I wish you could see all the boys and me
Doing loops and dives in tight formation
Chasing the wind
Like eagles in the sun"

It was spring again when I went to meet his train
They sent him home a hero
With medals and that look in his eyes
And a cane—
I hardly knew him
And most nights he'd wake up shaking and scared
But he'd never tell me what
He was seeing

But it was the spring of '45
It was such a hopeful time
When he was finally on the mend
We'd sit on the porch
And he'd watch the sky
Like he was looking for something

Oh flying
Sun on the silver wing
It's so silent out there
Like a blue cathedral
You can climb and climb
Till the earth falls away
And you're finally alone now
You've finally come home

Well the doctors told him he could never fly again
But a hero's a hero
And the air force takes care of its own
Oh they let him fly a desk for thirty years
And except for the drinking
Nothing much has changed
Ah he's still got his medals and his aches and pains
Still got his bad dreams

Ah he's still the same stranger I met
At the train

But there was a boy in '44
He always talked of flying
And one day his plane took off
And you know, they've never come down
They're still somewhere flying

Oh flying
Sun on the silver wing . . .

Mary Lynn Hammond
from the Stringband record,
Thanks to the Following

Flying a Red Kite

The ride home began badly. Still almost a stranger to the city, tired, hot and dirty, and inattentive to his surroundings, Fred stood for ten minutes, shifting his parcels from arm to arm and his weight from one leg to the other, in a sweaty bath of shimmering glare from the sidewalk, next to a grimy yellow-and-black bus stop. To his left a line of murmuring would-be passengers lengthened until there were enough to fill any vehicle that might come for them. Finally an obese brown bus waddled up like an indecent old cow and stopped with an expiring moo at the head of the line. Fred was glad to be first in line, as there didn't seem to be room for more than a few to embus.

But as he stepped up he noticed a sign in the window which said *Côte des Neiges-Boulevard* and he recoiled as though bitten, trampling the toes of the woman behind him and making her squeal. It was a Sixty-six bus, not the Sixty-five that he wanted. The woman pushed furiously past him while the remainder of the line clamoured in the rear. He stared at the number on the bus stop: Sixty-six, not his stop at all. Out of the corner of his eye he saw another coach pulling away from the stop on the northeast corner, the right stop, the Sixty-five, and the one he should have been standing under all this time. Giving his characteristic weary put-upon sigh, which he used before breakfast to annoy Naomi, he adjusted his parcels in both arms, feeling sweat run around his neck and down his collar between his shoulders, and crossed Saint Catherine against the light, drawing a Gallic sneer from a policeman, to stand for several more minutes at the head of a new queue, under the right sign. It was nearly 4.30 and the Saturday shopping crowds wanted to get home, out of the summer dust and heat, out of the jitter of the big July holiday weekend. They would all go home and sit on their balconies. All over the suburbs in duplexes and fourplexes, families would be enjoying cold suppers in the open air on their balconies; but the Calverts' apartment had none. Fred and Naomi had been ignorant of the meaning of the custom when they were apartment hunting. They had thought of Montreal as a city of the Sub-Arctic and in the summers they would have leisure to repent the misjudgement.

He had been shopping along the length of Saint Catherine between Peel and Guy, feeling guilty because he had heard for years that this was where all those pretty Montreal women made their prom-

enade; he had wanted to watch without familial encumbrances. There had been girls enough but nothing outrageously special so he had beguiled the scorching afternoon making a great many small idle purchases, of the kind one does when trapped in a Woolworth's. A ball-point pen and a note-pad for Naomi, who was always stealing his and leaving it in the kitchen with long, wildly-optimistic, grocery lists scribbled in it. Six packages of cigarettes, some legal-size envelopes, two Dinky-toys, a long-playing record, two parcels of second-hand books, and the lightest of his burdens and the unhandiest, the kite he had bought for Deedee, two flimsy wooden sticks rolled up in red plastic film, and a ball of cheap thin string—not enough, by the look of it, if he should ever get the thing into the air.

When he'd gone fishing, as a boy, he'd never caught any fish; when playing hockey he had never been able to put the puck in the net. One by one the wholesome outdoor sports and games had defeated him. But he had gone on believing in them, in their curative moral values, and now he hoped that Deedee, though a girl, might sometime catch a fish; and though she obviously wouldn't play hockey, she might ski, or toboggan on the mountain. He had noticed that people treated kites and kite-flying as somehow holy. They were a natural symbol, thought Fred, and he felt uneasily sure that he would have trouble getting this one to fly.

The inside of the bus was shaped like a box-car with windows, but the windows were useless. You might have peeled off the bus as you'd peel the paper off a pound of butter, leaving an oblong yellow lump of thick solid heat, with the passengers embedded in it like hopeless bread-crumbs.

He elbowed and wriggled his way along the aisle, feeling a momentary sliver of pleasure as his palm rubbed accidentally along the back of a girl's skirt—once, a philosopher—the sort of thing you couldn't be charged with. But you couldn't get away with it twice and anyway the girl either didn't feel it, or had no idea who had caressed her. There were vacant seats towards the rear, which was odd because the bus was otherwise full, and he struggled towards them, trying not to break the wooden struts which might be persuaded to fly. The bus lurched forward and his feet moved with the floor, causing him to pop suddenly out of the crowd by the exit, into a square well of space next to the heat and stink of the engine. He swayed around and aimed himself at a narrow vacant seat, nearly dropping a parcel of books as he lowered himself precipitately into it.

The bus crossed Sherbrooke Street and began, intolerably slowly, to crawl up Côte des Neiges and around the western spur of the mountain. His ears began to pick up the usual melange of French and English and to sort it out; he was proud of his French and pleased that most of the people on the streets spoke a less correct, though more fluent, version than his own. He had found that he could make his customers understand him perfectly—he was a book salesman—but that people on the street were happier when he addressed them in English.

The chatter in the bus grew clearer and more interesting and he began to listen, grasping all at once why he had found a seat back here. He was sitting next to a couple of drunks who emitted an almost overpowering smell of beer. They were cheerfully exchanging indecencies and obscure jokes and in a minute they would speak to him. They always did, drunks and panhandlers, finding some soft fearfulness in his face which exposed him as a shrinking easy mark. Once in a railroad station he had been approached three times in twenty minutes by the same panhandler on his rounds. Each time he had given the man something, despising himself with each new weakness.

The cheerful pair sitting at right angles to him grew louder and more blunt and the women within earshot grew glum. There was no harm in it; there never is. But you avoid your neighbour's eye, afraid of smiling awkwardly, or of looking offended and a prude.

"Now this Pearson," said one of the revellers, "he's just a little short-ass. He's just a little fellow without any brains. Why, some of the speeches he makes . . . I could make them myself. I'm an old Tory myself, an old Tory."

"I'm an old Blue," said the other.

"Is that so, now? That's fine, a fine thing." Fred was sure he didn't know what a Blue was.

"I'm a Balliol man. Whoops!" They began to make monkey-like noises to annoy the passengers and amuse themselves. "Whoops," said the Oxford man again, "hoo, hoo, there's one now, there's one for you." He was talking about a girl on the sidewalk.

"She's a one, now, isn't she? Look at the legs on her, oh, look at them now, isn't that something?" There was a noisy clearing of throats and the same voice said something that sounded like "Shaoil-na-baig."

"Oh, good, good!" said the Balliol man.

"Shaoil-na-baig," said the other loudly, "I've not forgotten my Gaelic, do you see, shaoil-na-baig," he said it loudly, and a woman up the aisle reddened and looked away. It sounded like a dirty phrase to Fred, delivered as though the speaker had forgotten all his Gaelic but the words for sexual intercourse.

"And how is your French, Father?" asked the Balliol man, and the title made Fred start in his seat. He pretended to drop a parcel and craned his head quickly sideways. The older of the two drunks, the one sitting by the window, examining the passing legs and skirts with the same impulse that Fred had felt on Saint Catherine Street, was indeed a priest, and couldn't possibly be an impostor. His clerical suit was too well-worn, egg-stained and blemished with candle-droppings, and fit its wearer too well, for it to be an assumed costume. The face was unmistakably a southern Irishman's. The priest darted a quick peek into Fred's eyes before he could turn them away, giving a monkey-like grimace that might have been a mixture of embarrassment and shame but probably wasn't.

He was a little gray-haired bucko of close to sixty, with a triangular sly mottled crimson face and uneven yellow teeth. His hands moved jerkily and expressively in his lap, in counterpoint to the lively intelligent movements of his face.

The other chap, the Balliol man, was a perfect type of English-speaking Montrealer, perhaps a bond salesman or minor functionary in a brokerage house on Saint James Street. He was about fifty with a round domed head, red hair beginning to go slightly white at the neck and ears, pink porcine skin, very neatly barbered and combed. He wore an expensive white shirt with a fine blue stripe and there was some sort of ring around his tie. He had his hands folded fatly on the knob of a stick, round face with deep laugh-lines in the cheeks, and a pair of cheerfully darting little blue-bloodshot eyes. Where could the pair have run into each other?

"I've forgotten my French years ago," said the priest carelessly. "I was down in New Brunswick for many years and I'd no use for it, the work I was doing. I'm Irish, you know."

"I'm an old Blue."

"That's right," said the priest, "John's the boy. Oh, he's a sharp lad is John. He'll let them all get off, do you see, to Manitoba for the summer, and bang, BANG!" All the bus jumped. "He'll call an election on them and then they'll run." Something caught his eye and he turned to gaze out the window. The bus was moving slowly past the cemetery of Notre Dame des Neiges and the priest stared, half-sober, at the graves stretched up the mountainside in the sun.

"I'm not in there," he said involuntarily.

"Indeed you're not," said his companion, "lots of life in you yet, eh, Father?"

"Oh," he said, "oh, I don't think I'd know what to do with a girl if I fell over one." He looked out at the cemetery for several moments. "It's all a sham," he said, half under his breath, "they're in there for good." He swung around and looked innocently at Fred. "Are you going fishing, lad?"

"It's a kite that I bought for my little girl," said Fred, more cheerfully than he felt.

"She'll enjoy that, she will," said the priest, "for it's grand sport."

"Go fly a kite!" said the Oxford man hilariously. It amused him and he said it again. "Go fly a kite! " He and the priest began to chant together, "Hoo, hoo, whoops," and they laughed and in a moment, clearly, would begin to sing.

The bus turned lumberingly onto Queen Mary Road. Fred stood up confusedly and began to push his way towards the rear door. As he turned away, the priest grinned impudently at him, stammering a jolly goodbye. Fred was too embarrassed to answer but he smiled uncertainly and fled. He heard them take up their chant anew.

"Hoo, there's a one for you, hoo. Shaoil-na-baig. Whoops!" Their laughter died out as the bus rolled heavily away.

He had heard about such men, naturally, and knew that they existed; but it was the first time in Fred's life that he had ever seen a priest misbehave himself publicly. There are so many priests in the city, he thought, that the number of bum ones must be in proportion. The explanation satisfied him but the incident left a disagreeable impression in his mind.

Safely home he took his shirt off and poured himself a Coke. Then he allowed Deedee, who was dancing around him with her terrible energy, to open the parcels.

"Give your Mummy the pad and pencil, sweetie," he directed. She crossed obediently to Naomi's chair and handed her the cheap plastic case.

"Let me see you make a note in it," he said, "make a list of something, for God's sake, so you'll remember it's yours. And the one on the desk is mine. Got that?" He spoke without rancour or much interest; it was a rather overworked joke between them.

"What's this?" said Deedee, holding up the kite

and allowing the ball of string to roll down the hall. He resisted a compulsive wish to get up and re-wind the string.

"It's for you. Don't you know what it is?"

"It's a red kite," she said. She had wanted one for weeks but spoke now as if she weren't interested. Then all at once she grew very excited and eager. "Can you put it together right now?" she begged.

"I think we'll wait till after supper, sweetheart," he said, feeling mean. You raised their hopes and then dashed them; there was no real reason why they shouldn't put it together now, except his fatigue. He looked pleadingly at Naomi.

"Daddy's tired, Deedee," she said obligingly, "he's had a long hot afternoon."

"But I want to see it," said Deedee, fiddling with the flimsy red film and nearly puncturing it.

Fred was sorry he'd drunk a Coke; it bloated him and upset his stomach and had no true cooling effect.

"We'll have something to eat," he said cajolingly, "and then Mummy can put it together for you." He turned to his wife. "You don't mind, do you? I'd only spoil the thing." Threading a needle or hanging a picture made the normal slight tremor of his hands accentuate itself almost embarrassingly.

"Of course not," she said, smiling wryly. They had long ago worked out their areas of uselessness.

"There's a picture on it, and directions."

"Yes. Well, we'll get it together somehow. Flying it . . . that's something else again." She got up, holding the notepad, and went into the kitchen to put the supper on.

It was a good hot-weather supper, tossed greens with the correct proportions of vinegar and oil, croissants and butter, and cold sliced ham. As he ate, his spirits began to percolate a bit, and he gave Naomi a graphic sketch of the incident on the bus. "It depressed me," he told her. This came as no surprise to her; almost anything unusual, which he couldn't do anything to alter or relieve, depressed Fred nowadays. "He must have been sixty. Oh, quite sixty, I should think, and you could tell that everything had come to pieces for him."

"It's a standard story," she said, "and aren't you sentimentalizing it?"

"In what way?"

"The 'spoiled priest' business, the empty man, the man without a calling. They all write about that. Graham Greene made his whole career out of that."

"That isn't what the phrase means," said Fred

laboriously. "It doesn't refer to a man who actually *is* a priest, though without a vocation."

"No?" She lifted an eyebrow; she was better educated than he.

"No, it doesn't. It means somebody who never became a priest at all. The point is that you *had* a vocation but ignored it. That's what a spoiled priest is. It's an Irish phrase, and usually refers to somebody who is a failure and who drinks too much." He laughed shortly. "I don't qualify, on the second count."

"You're not a failure."

"No, I'm too young. Give me time!" There was no reason for him to talk like this; he was a very productive salesman.

"You certainly never wanted to be a priest," she said positively, looking down at her breasts and laughing, thinking of some secret. "I'll bet you never considered it, not with your habits." She meant his bedroom habits, which were ardent, and in which she ardently acquiesced. She was an adept and enthusiastic partner, her greatest gift as a wife.

"Let's put that kite together," said Deedee, getting up from her little table, with such adult decision that her parents chuckled. "Come on," she said, going to the sofa and bouncing up and down.

Naomi put a tear in the fabric right away, on account of the ambiguity of the directions. There should have been two holes in the kite, through which a lugging-string passed; but the holes hadn't been provided and when she put them there with the point of an icepick they immediately began to grow.

"Scotch tape," she said, like a surgeon asking for sutures.

"There's a picture on the front," said Fred, secretly cross but ostensibly helpful.

"I see it," she said.

"Mummy put holes in the kite," said Deedee with alarm. "Is she going to break it?"

"No," said Fred. The directions were certainly ambiguous.

Naomi tied the struts at right-angles, using so much string that Fred was sure the kite would be too heavy. Then she strung the fabric on the notched ends of the struts and the thing began to take shape.

"It doesn't look quite right," she said, puzzled and irritated.

"The surface has to be curved so there's a difference of air pressure." He remembered this, rather unfairly, from high-school physics classes.

She bent the cross-piece and tied it in a bowed arc, and the red film pulled taut. "There now," she said.

"You've forgotten the lugging-string on the front," said Fred critically, "that's what you made the holes for, remember?"

"Why is Daddy mad?" said Deedee.

"I'M NOT MAD!"

It had begun to shower, great pear-shaped drops of rain falling with a plop on the sidewalk.

"That's as close as I can come," said Naomi, staring at Fred, "we aren't going to try it tonight, are we?"

"We promised her," he said, "and it's only a light rain."

"Will we all go?"

"I wish you'd take her," he said, "because my stomach feels upset. I should never drink Coca-Cola."

"It always bothers you. You should know that by now."

"I'm not running out on you," he said anxiously, "and if you can't make it work, I'll take her up tomorrow afternoon."

"I know," she said, "come on, Deedee, we're going to take the kite up the hill." They left the house and crossed the street. Fred watched them through the window as they started up the steep path hand in hand. He felt left out, and slightly nauseated.

They were back in half an hour, their spirits not at all dampened, which surprised him.

"No go, eh?"

"Much too wet, and not enough breeze. The rain knocks it flat."

"O.K.!" he exclaimed with fervour. "I'll try tomorrow."

"We'll try again tomorrow," said Deedee with equal determination—her parents mustn't forget their obligations.

Sunday afternoon the weather was nearly perfect, hot, clear, a firm steady breeze but not too much of it, and a cloudless sky. At two o'clock Fred took his daughter by the hand and they started up the mountain together, taking the path through the woods that led up to the university parking lots.

"We won't come down until we make it fly," Fred swore, "that's a promise."

"Good," she said, hanging on to his hand and letting him drag her up the steep path, "there are lots of bugs in here, aren't there?"

"Yes," he said briefly—he was being liberally bitten.

When they came to the end of the path, they saw that the campus was deserted and still, and there was all kinds of running room. Fred gave Deedee careful instructions about where to sit, and what to do if a car should come along, and then he paid out a little string and began to run across the parking lot towards the main building of the university. He felt a tug at the string and throwing a glance over his shoulder he saw the kite bobbing in the air, about twenty feet off the ground. He let out more string, trying to keep it filled with air, but he couldn't run quite fast enough, and in a moment it fell back to the ground.

"Nearly had it!" he shouted to Deedee, whom he'd left fifty yards behind.

"Daddy, Daddy, come back," she hollered apprehensively. Rolling up the string as he went, he retraced his steps and prepared to try again. It was important to catch a gust of wind and run into it. On the second try the kite went higher than before but as he ran past the entrance to the university he felt the air pressure lapse and saw the kite waver and fall. He walked slowly back, realizing that the bulk of the main building was cutting off the air currents.

"We'll go up higher," he told her, and she seized his hand and climbed obediently up the road beside him, around behind the main building, past ash barrels and trash heaps; they climbed a flight of wooden steps, crossed a parking lot next to L'Ecole Polytechnique and a slanting field further up, and at last came to a pebbly dirt road that ran along the top ridge of the mountain beside the cemetery. Fred remembered the priest as he looked across the fence and along the broad stretch of cemetery land rolling away down the slope of the mountain to the west. They were about six hundred feet above the river, he judged. He'd never been up this far before.

"My sturdy little brown legs are tired," Deedee remarked, and he burst out laughing.

"Where did you hear that," he said, "who has sturdy little brown legs?"

She screwed her face up in a grin. "The gingerbread man," she said, beginning to sing, "I can run away from you, I can, 'cause I'm the little gingerbread man."

The air was dry and clear and without a trace of humidity and the sunshine was dazzling. On either side of the dirt road grew great clumps of wild flowers, yellow and blue, buttercups, daisies and goldenrod, and cornflowers and clover. Deedee disappeared into the flowers—picking bouquets was her favourite game. He could see the shrubs and grasses heave and sway as she moved around. The scent of clover and of dry sweet grass was very keen here, and from the east, over the curved top of the mountain, the wind blew in a steady uneddying stream. Five or six miles off to the southwest he spied the wide intensely gray-white stripe of the river. He heard Deedee cry: "Daddy, Daddy, come and look." He pushed through the coarse grasses and found her.

"Berries," she cried rapturously, "look at all the berries! Can I eat them?" She had found a wild raspberry bush, a thing he hadn't seen since he was six years old. He'd never expected to find one growing in the middle of Montreal.

"Wild raspberries," he said wonderingly, "sure you can pick them dear; but be careful of the prickles." They were all shades and degrees of ripeness from black to vermilion.

"Ouch," said Deedee, pricking her fingers as she pulled off the berries. She put a handful in her mouth and looked wry.

"Are they bitter?"

"Juicy," she mumbled with her mouth full. A trickle of dark juice ran down her chin.

"Eat some more," he said, "while I try the kite again." She bent absorbedly to the task of hunting them out, and he walked down the road for some distance and then turned to run up towards her. This time he gave the kite plenty of string before he began to move; he ran as hard as he could, panting and handing the string out over his shoulders, burning his fingers as it slid through them. All at once he felt the line pull and pulse as if there were a living thing on the other end and he turned on his heel and watched while the kite danced into the upper air-currents above the treetops and began to soar up and up. He gave it more line and in an instant it pulled high up away from him across the fence, two hundred feet and more above him up over the cemetery where it steadied and hung, bright red in the sunshine. He thought flashingly of the priest saying "It's all a sham," and he knew all at once that the priest was wrong. Deedee came running down to him, laughing with excitement and pleasure and singing joyfully about the gingerbread man, and he knelt in the dusty roadway and put his arms around her, placing her hands on the line between his. They gazed, squinting in the sun, at the flying red thing, and he turned away and saw in the shadow of her cheek and on her lips and chin the dark rich red of the pulp and juice of the crushed raspberries.

Hugh Hood

It's in the Egg IN THE LITTLE ROUND EGG

We are continually bored with the air,
the round doors, the flat tables, the straight spoons,
the whole damned breakfast ritual, the toast floating in the air
and suspended above our heads and the egg, the little round egg,
the paranoid egg, laid by the round hen in isolation;
the egg, the hen, fertilized by unnatural forces,
the light, the ultra blue light working
first on the bird and
then the egg, the little round egg balanced
on its little bottom
on our square plates.
and now the impression of tiny fingers working
at the top or the bottom
of the egg, always the round egg—
and our fingers, our precise fingers
digging, probing the round egg
like a conspiracy
like the egg contained the secret of the Sunday bomb.
it's in the egg
in the yolk of the egg;
the little plans
the final solution for the human race
it's in the
yolk.

And now I can see it
the blue light working on us,
urging us to tell everything,
all our intimate living,
the colour of our bank accounts;
details, details, details,
it's in
the
yolk.

And now all our fingers work furiously,
all six tiny fingers probing, digging
deeper, deeper,
into the guts of the egg.
it's in the egg in the yolk of the egg in the yolk
of the egg in the yolk of the egg in the yolk—
                    of the little round egg.

We are continually bored with the air, the round doors, the flat tables, the
straight spoons, the whole damned breakfast ritual, the toast floating in the
air and suspended above our heads, the golden brown toast, the delirious sunny
toast, the toast begging to be anointed with margarine, the toast dipped in
the yolk of the egg, in the yolk that tells all.

Joe Rosenblatt

The Black Fly Song

1. TWAS EAR-LY IN THE SPRING WHEN I DE-CIDE TO GO FOR TO WORK UP IN THE WOODS IN NORTH ON-TA-RI-O, AND THE UN-EM-PLOY-MENT OF-FICE SAID THEY'D SEND ME THROUGH TO THE LIT-TLE A-BI-TI-BI WITH THE SUR-VEY CREW.

AND THE BLACK FLIES THE LIT-TLE BLACK FLIES, AL-WAYS THE BLACK-FLY NO MAT-TER WHERE YOU GO, I'LL DIE WITH THE BLACK-FLY A-PIC-KIN' MY BONES IN — NORTH ON-TA-RI-O, I-O, IN — NORTH ON-TA-RI-O.

Now the man Black Toby was the captain of the crew
And he said: "I'm gonna tell you boys what we're gonna
They want to build a power dam and we must find a way
For to make the Little Ab flow around the other way."

So we survey to the east and we survey to the west
And we couldn't make our minds up how to do it best.
Little Ab, Little Ab, what shall I do?
For I'm all but goin' crazy on the survey crew.

It was black fly, black fly everywhere,
a-crawlin' in your whiskers, a-crawlin' in your hair;
A-swimmin' in the soup and a-swimmin' in the tea;
Oh the devil take the black fly and let me be.

Black Toby fell to swearin' 'cause the work went slow.
And the state of our morale was gettin' pretty low,
And the flies swarmed heavy—it was hard to catch a bre
As you staggered up and down the trail talkin' to yourse

Now the bull cook's name was Blind River Joe;
If it hadn't been for him we'd've never pulled through
For he bound up our bruises, and he kidded us for fun,
And he lathered us with bacon grease and balsam gum.

At last the job was over; Black Toby said: "We're throug
With the Little Abitibi and the survey crew."
'Twas a wonderful experience and this I know
I'll never go again to North Ontar-i-o.

Wade Hemsworth

30

Lark Song

If we'd of been smart we never would have let Joseph go off by himself that Saturday in Wetaskiwin. But we did, and there sure been a lot of trouble for everybody ever since. My brother, Joseph Ermineskin, be older than me. He is twenty-two already, but when he just a baby he catch the scarlet fever and his mind it never grow up like his body do.

Joseph ain't crazy. He just got a tiny kid's mind in a big man's body. He is close to six feet tall and broad across the shoulder. His face is round and the colour of varnished wood. He be gentle and never hurt nobody in his whole life.

Unless you look right in his eyes he don't look no different than the rest of us guys. We let his hair grow long, and we got him a denim outfit, and once when I worked at a mine for the summer, I bought him a pair of cowboy boots. But Joseph he smile too often and too long at a time. I guess it because his mind ain't full of worries like everybody else.

Joseph ain't no more trouble to look after than any other little kid and he is even good at a couple of things. He can hear a song on the radio and then play it back on my old guitar just like he heard it. He forget it pretty quick though, and can usually only do it one time.

And he can sound like birds. He caws like the crows so good that they come to see where the crow is that's talking to them. He talk like a magpie too, but best of all he sound like a meadowlark. Meadowlarks make the prettiest sound of any bird I ever heard, when they sing it sound like sweet water come bubble up out of a spring.

Sometime when we sit around the cabin at night and everyone is sad, Joseph he make that lark song for us and soon everyone is feel some better because it so pretty.

It is funny that he can do that sound so good, 'cause when he talk he sound like the wind-up record player when it not cranked up good enough. His voice is all slow and funny and he have to stop a long time between words.

One time, Papa, when he still lived here with us, is take Joseph with him to Wetaskiwin. Papa he get drunk and don't come home for a week or so, but the very next day, Joseph he is show up. He is hungry and tired from walk all those miles down the highway, but he find his way home real good. He is smile clear around to the back of his neck when he see us, and he don't ask about go to town with anybody for a long time after that.

Still I can tell he feel bad when me and my friend Frank Fence-post and all the guys go into town in Louis Coyote's pickup truck and leave him at home. That was why we take him one Saturday afternoon with us. We put him in the park to play while we go look in the stores and maybe stop for a beer or two. Joseph sure like the swings, and being strong and tall he can sure swing up high. What we should of told him though, and didn't, was for sure not to play with none of them white kids.

White people don't like nobody else to touch their kids, especially Indians. Here on the reserve it's kind of like one family, the kids run free when they is little and nobody minds if somebody else hugs your little boy or girl.

Joseph he like little kids and they like him back. Big people don't always have time, or maybe they don't want to, love their kids as much as they should. Joseph is pick up the kids when they fall down, or maybe when they is just lonesome. He don't say nothing to them, just pet their heads like maybe they was little kittens, hold them close and make them feel warm. Sometimes he make his bird sounds for them, and they forget why they feel bad, hug his neck, and feel good that someone likes them.

People say that was what happen in the park in Wetaskiwin that day. A little white girl is fall off the slide and hurt herself. When Joseph see her crying he is just pick her up like he would an Indian kid. Only them kids all been told, don't mess around with strangers, and somebody runs for some mothers.

We come back to get Joseph about the same time that little girl's mother come to get her. If you ever seen a lady partridge fly around on the ground pretend she got a broken wing so her enemy go after her and leave her young ones alone, that is how that white lady is act.

Joseph is just stand in the sandbox hold that little girl in his arms, and she is not even crying anymore until she hear her mother scream and dance up and down. I sure afraid for what might have happen to Joseph if we don't come when we did.

I unwrap his arms from the little girl and hand her back to the lady, who is cry some and yell a lot of bad things at us and say somebody already called the RCMP.

The RCMP guys come roll up in their car with the lights flash and I sure wish we was all someplace else. While everyone try to yell louder than everyone else, Joseph he sit down and play some in the sand and every once in a while he is make his meadowlark call.

I try to explain to them RCMP guys that Joseph he is about as harmless as that meadowlark he is sounding like. Meadowlarks ain't very pretty or good for much but make beautiful sounds, but they sure don't hurt nobody either, I tell them.

Lots of people is standing around watching and I think they figure something real bad has happened. There is a real big white lady with a square face is carry a shotgun.

We promise the RCMP guys and anybody else that will listen that for sure we never gonna bring Joseph to town no more. We keep him on the reserve forever and then some, we tell them.

For once it look like maybe the RCMP is gonna believe us Indians. They say they can't see no reason to lay any charges, 'cause all it look like Joseph done was to pick up a kid that fall down. The white girl's mother is yell loud on everybody, say if the RCMP ain't gonna do nothing she'll go to somebody who will. And that lady with the square face wave her shotgun and say she would sure like to shoot herself a few wagon-burners.

After we all go to the police station for a while the RCMP guys let us take Joseph home, but it is only a couple of days until some Government people is come nose around our place a lot. They is kind of like the coyotes come pick at the garbage, we hardly ever see them but we still know they is there.

Two little women in brown suits come to our cabin, say wouldn't we think Joseph be happier in a home someplace where there are lots of other retarded guys.

Ma, like she always do, pretend she don't understand English, and just sit and look at them with a stone face. But she sure is worried.

Next time they come back, they ain't nearly so nice. They say either we put Joseph in the place for crazy people at Ponoka, or they get a judge to tell us we have to.

The next week, me and my girlfriend Sadie One-wound, hitch-hike the twelve miles down to Ponoka to have a look at the crazy place. I know all my life that the place is there but there is something about a place like that that scares us a lot. It make us too shy to go up to the gate and ask to look around. Instead we just walk around outside for a while. It got big high wire fences but inside there is lots of grass and beds of pretty flowers, and the people who walk around inside don't look as though they trying to run away or nothing.

The Government peoples keep sending Ma big fat letters with red writing on them. One say that

Ma and Joseph got to appear at something called a committal hearing at the court room in Wetaskiwin. We figure that if we go there they gonna take Joseph away from us for sure.

I go down to the pay phone at Hobbema Crossing and phone all the way to Calgary to the office of Mr. William Wuttunee, the Indian lawyer, but he is away on holiday, and no, I say, I don't want nobody to call me or nothing.

We don't go to that committal hearing 'cause Ma, she say that we just pretend that nothing is happening, and if we do that long enough the white people stop bothering us.

A couple of weeks later we get another big bunch of papers with red seals all over them, delivered by the RCMP guys personal. Them papers say they gonna come and get Joseph on a certain date. We figure it out on the calendar from the Texaco service station, and we decide that when they come they ain't gonna find no Joseph. We just put him to live with someone back in the bush a few miles and move him around whenever we have to.

One good thing about white people is that they usually give up easy. The RCMP is always nose around for Sam Standing-at-the-door's still, or maybe have a warrant for arrest somebody for steal car parts or something, but we rear up the culvert in the road from Hobbema to our cabins, and them guys sure hate to walk much, so they just go away after they yell at the closest Indians for a while. We figure the Government people like to walk even less than the RCMP so it be pretty easy to fool them.

I don't know if they came a day early or if maybe we forget a day someplace, but their cars is already across the culvert and halfway up the hill before we see them. And the guy from the crazy place in Ponoka, who wears a white jacket, look like he be a cook in a café, say he is a Métis, and he even talk Cree to us, which is real bad, 'cause then we can't pretend we don't understand what is happening. Usually, people we don't like go away real quick when we pretend we don't understand, especially if we sharpen a knife or play with a gun while we talk about them some in our language.

This Métis guy tell us, look, they ain't gonna hurt Joseph down there at the mental hospital, and it only be twelve miles away so we can come visit him anytime. He gonna be warm and clean and have lots of food and he get to make friends with other guys like him and maybe even learn to make things with his hands and stuff.

It don't sound so bad after all, if it true what he

says. All we had time to do was hide Joseph under the big bed in the cabin, and he been making bird songs all the time he is under there. Ma, she finally call him to come out, and he poke out his head and smile on everybody.

We pack up his clothes in a cardboard box. He sure ain't got much to take with him. Frank Fencepost ask them guys if they got electric light down at the crazy place, and they tell him the hospital is fully equipped. Frank he goes and gets his fancy-shaped electric guitar that he bought at a pawnshop in Calgary. He tell the guys from the hospital they should show Joseph how to plug the guitar into the wall. Then he shove the guitar into Joseph's arms.

The kids is all come out from the cabins and stand around look shy at the ground while I talk to Joseph, like I would my little sister, explain he should be good, and how these guys is his friends and all. Joseph he pet the guitar like it alive and smile for everybody and touch his fingers on the shiny paint of the car from Ponoka.

Once they is gone we sure ain't got much to say to each other. Me and Frank talk a little about how we go visit Joseph on Saturday, sneak him away and hide him out on the reserve. But it different when they got him than when we got him, and I don't think that idea ever gonna come to much.

I don't sleep so good that night. I am up early. The sky is clear and the sun is just come up. There is frost on the brown grasses and the slough at the foot of the hill is frozen thin as if window glass had been laid across it. Brown bulrushes tipped with frost, stand, some straight, some at angles, like spears been stuck in the ground. Outside the cabin door our dogs lie curled like horse collars in their dirt nests. They half open their yellow eyes, look at me then go to sleep again. The air is thin and clear and pine smoke from another cabin is rise straight up like ink lines on paper. From the woodpile I carry up an armful of split pine. The wood is cold on my arm and I tuck the last piece under my chin.

Then there is like an explosion from down the hill and across the slough someplace. Like a gun shot, only beautiful. The crows rise up like they been tossed out of the spruce trees.

At first I want to laugh it sound so funny, the voice of a summer bird on a frosty morning. Then it come again, that sweet, bubbly, blue-sky-coloured lark song. I do laugh then, but for happy, and I toss the wood on the ground and run for the meadow.

W.P. Kinsella

The Mouth Organ Symphony

You ever heard a symphony made up of mouth organs? No, and you never will now. I think the mouth organ is gone for good, but in the hard times, on the road, it was one of our best friends. I remember once near Hamilton about 100 of us were in the basement for a factory or something which had stopped being built because of the hard times. The country was full of basements like that.

We'd been picking fruit. I remember it was in the fall and there were about five fires going and everybody had a bit of money and was cooking stew or warming up cans of stuff and there was a good-time feeling. It got dark and soon everybody was around one big fire in the middle, about a hundred guys, I'd reckon, and everybody full of food and passing the rollings around and one guy brought out his harmonica and that's the fancy name for a mouth organ. He started to play, and Christ, that man was good, and everybody soon stopped talking.

We always used to talk about what the government was doing, and how we were being screwed and where jobs were and where we had this terrific meal, things like that. Food was always important to us. Funny, but women weren't. I guess we just didn't have the energy. Besides, there were no women.

Anyway, there was this guy with the mouth organ and soon another guy brought one out and another until there were about ten. Now, remember, I guess not two of these guys had ever played together before. But it was as if they had played together for years, and remember you can buy a harmonica for a lot of money or a cheap one for a buck or two, but when they were all together quality or price didn't mean a hoot. I guess you could say they were inspired, and that's why I asked if you had ever heard a symphony of mouth organs.

They played for about two hours, and I guess every guy there was thinking of home, of mother, sweethearts, brothers and sisters, sitting around the tree opening Christmas presents, sleigh rides, the way the creek made a loop and the water was warm and soft for swimming, the smell of bacon and eggs and stewed tomatoes for Sunday breakfast and walking over crisp snow with a twenty-two looking for rabbits with your dog running ahead, bouncing around. These were the things I was thinking about, so that's why I mention them. We were all thinking of home. The good days. The other times.

They played songs like "Mother Macree" and "There's A Long, Long Trail A-winding" and "I'll Take You Home Again, Kathleen" and "Flow Gently, Sweet Afton" and "Girl Of My Dreams" and an awful lot of others. Some we sang, some we just kept quiet. Nobody said we'd sing one and not another. It just happened, you see. Songs, of course, you never hear today. The old songs. Good ones, I'll tell you.

That was the night when the fruit picking was over, except for some cleaning up, and so everybody went his own way next morning and I've of-ten wondered after that night how many decided to chuck the life on the road, this moving from town to town, and go back home. If they could find it. I know I did, but I didn't go home. I just kept going and going because there was absolutely nothing at home for me. I would just have been another mouth to feed, and I would have been taking food out of the mouths of the little ones. So I just kept on going. I was seventeen at the time.

as told to Barry Broadfoot in
Ten Lost Years

Music

In the middle
of the afternoon
in the next apartment
                              people I've
                              never met
are playing music
loud and vigorous
                    the kind
you can dance to

I suppose they're not aware
of the noise they're making
                              people having fun
                              rarely are

But I have rights as well
and am about to knock on their door
when I catch myself:
                    you old man
you're only afraid of their
life
      because you have so little
Listen to them
Hear their voices

And thinking back
                    I realize
I do know them
                    We met as
children in a game
                    We played with music
for we knew that of everything
around us
                music alone
had no end

David Bittle

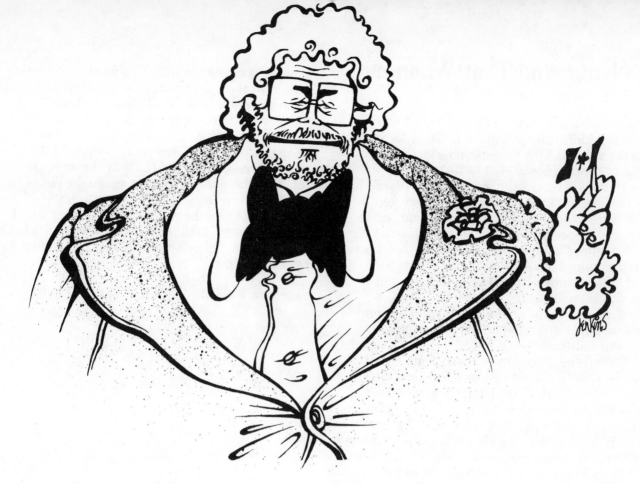

Flowers for Lightfoot

You were the music man
a feeling couched in sound
sighs in homespun
wishes stretched along singing strings
pain in a deep timbre

You were the stageheld man
rounded slim neck holy in hand
plucking taut strings of guitar hearts
fingering frets of a few
like you

You were the man of the empty bottle
facing the night in winter

Changes   And blood-dipped eyes
speak of the pain not of passion
but of passion lost

Old lines
tired now
spring gone
slip from hollow rosewood box
of yesterweeping sound
Hands without arms
noisy in unison

beget brand new
old lines
life notes traded
for the flash
of a thousand bulbs
and an echo
of applause

The pillars of home in Massey Hall
which have always stood for you
now stretch in stolid hurt reproach
The drained bottle by your bed
mouths a friend's betrayal

Music man   where do you go now
after the proud pained sweep off stage
when the claps are a brain smack
a flap trap for air

Where do you go
when the lined and secret parts of you
waiting in the wings
shrink at your approach

The songs of the future have been sung
You were one   You
were one

Dave Cavanagh

The King And That Woman

I never felt hard done by. You could say I was just a normal middle class girl living in Toronto. I went to school and I had my friends and I loved my parents, and because I was born in 1928 I really didn't know there was such a thing as the Depression. I know it now, but in such a superficial way you couldn't really count me in. I only remember one thing. The Prince of Wales. When he became king and Mrs. Simpson, who my father (who was a real United Empire Loyalist type and still is at 84) called "That woman from Baltimore." Do you think this is important?

Well, all right. The principal announced there would be a special assembly this particular morning in the auditorium, and it was the first I remember when all the classes were there, from the little ones up to the Grade 9s. I guess I was Grade 4. Or Grade 5? We all sat on the floor, these hundreds of kids and there was this radio up at the front on a table and the principal, God, what was that man's name? He told us that the king was going to make an important announcement at 10 o'clock by short wave from England and he sort of put us into the picture, this talk of the king and this Mrs. Simpson, the American. I can remember the way he spoke, that this Mrs. Simpson had to be the worst bitch that ever drew breath. Didn't say it of course, but even the Grade Ones must have got the picture. Even in my own small way I remember thinking, "The King of England going to marry *an American!*" Americans weren't very high on the scale in our family, in a lot of families in Toronto in those days. We loved the king, and I had pictures from magazines in my room of the young prince, you know, so handsome, riding a horse on his ranch in Alberta, inspecting a regiment, playing polo, and I guess you could say he was the darling of the world.

Now I just don't think he was very bright, I think that he let down his country and the Empire. Very badly. But enough, the man is dead now and I'm sorry.

His voice came over, quite clear. I mean we could hear the words clearly and the way he put it I don't think most of us realized just what he had said. I remember the part about the woman I love, or the woman I must have beside me to help bear the burdens. You know. Then the principal stood up again and a couple of women teachers were weeping, and that made quite an impression I must say, and the principal explained that we would soon have a new king, that he would be the old king's brother, the younger one. And then he asked us to stand and sing "God Save The King" and we did and I remember crying. Maybe it was because my own class teacher over by the wall, a lovely woman we all loved, she was crying, and then about three-quarters of the way through, the teacher who was playing the piano she put her head down on the keys and began to cry.

I think it was the most dramatic thing that I have ever seen. Looking back on it I think what a great movie those days would make and what he ever saw in her I'll never know.

as told to Barry Broadfoot in *Ten Lost Years*

The Price of Progress

Guglielmo Marconi received the first trans-Atlantic wireless message standing on a hilltop in St. John's, Newfoundland on Thursday, December 12, 1901. On the following Monday, December 16, the price of the stocks of the cable companies started to plummet. That Monday evening, Marconi was kicked out of Newfoundland by the Anglo-American Telegraph Company who claimed sole and exclusive rights to telegraph communication to and from the island. Big business could move fast when its interests were at stake.

But so could the Canadian government. It offered Marconi $80,000 to move his wireless operations to Glace Bay, Cape Breton Island, Nova Scotia, the money to be spent on construction of a wireless station that would join Canada to England. Marconi accepted the offer.

Although unable to claim Marconi as a native son, Canadians can boast an historical participation in a wireless communication system that has become one of the wonders of the world . . .

from *The Canadian Inventions Book*, by Janis Nostbakken and Jack Humphrey

The Broadcaster's Poem

I used to broadcast at night
alone in the radio station,
but I was never good at it,
partly because my voice wasn't right
but mostly because my peculiar
metaphysical stupidity
made it impossible
for me to keep believing
there was somebody listening
when it seemed I was talking
only to myself in a room no bigger
than an ordinary bathroom.
I could believe it for a while
but then I'd get somewhat
the same feeling as when you
start to suspect you're the victim
of a practical joke.
                That wasn't rational.
So one part of me was afraid
another part of me might blurt out
something about myself
so terrible that even I
had never until
that moment suspected it.
                That was like the fear
of bridges and other
high places: Will I take off my glasses
and throw them
into the water, although I'm
half-blind without them?
Will I sneak up behind
myself and push?
(I'm doing here in a game now
what I might have done
then in reality).
Another thing: as a reporter
I covered an accident in which a train
ran into a car, killing
three young men, one of whom
was beheaded. The bodies looked
boneless as such bodies do.
More like mounds of rags.
And inside the wreckage,
where nobody could get at it
to make it stop, the car radio
was still playing.
                I thought about the places
the disc jockey's voice goes
and the things that happen there
and how impossible it would be for him
to continue if he really knew.

Alden Nowlan

The Perils of Max

One of the most painful interviews I can remember doing on [CBC Halifax's television show] *Gazette* was with a lady called Mrs. Thomas. She had phoned one day and asked if she might come on the program to talk about ocelots, a variety of small leopard used in Venezuela for hunting. She arrived on the set that evening with a live ocelot on a leash. Having observed it for about ten minutes hissing, spitting, growling, and lunging at anyone who came within five feet of it, I was a bit uneasy when I learned that Mrs. Thomas planned to have it with her all through our interview. She assured me that it would lie quietly at our feet and to put my fears at rest, she had brought along a big bone, which she planned to give to the ocelot when the interview started.

Sure enough, the interview went quite smoothly, with the ocelot curled up contentedly, munching on its bone just beside my right foot. Mrs. Thomas was a charming personality. She was personable and knew her subject well. Certainly, what I could hear of her through the growls, bone splintering, and chop smacking coming up from the floor seemed most interesting. I think my mistake was in letting the interview run on longer than planned, because somewhere along the line the ocelot had finished tearing off all the edible portions of meat from the bone and was looking around for seconds. It was while he was in this restless mood that I happened to move my right foot, indicating to the ocelot, no doubt, that the object he'd seen out of the corner of his eye was indeed alive.

With an angry snarl he hurled himself at my ankle and, taking the whole thing in his jaws, crunched down hard. My first reaction to the excruciating pain was to reach down and pry off his jaws with my hands. Just as I made my lunge, Mrs. Thomas offered her memorable advice, "Oh, don't do that! You might make him angry." Like a fool I followed her advice and let him have his way with my ankle to preserve his "good natured" mood. Trying to ignore the pain, I pressed on with the interview, until the growls and slavering became so loud you could hardly hear our voices. By now the camera had "dollied in" for a close-up and our dinner-time viewers were treated to a charming shot, full screen, of the scarlet stain now oozing through and spreading over my light-coloured socks.

Mrs. Thomas, all the while, was offering advice, stressing that the most important thing was not to anger the ocelot, and that if we could just manage to ignore the little fellow, he'd soon tire of his attention-getting behaviour. Since the ocelot gave no indication that he would tire much before he'd worked his way up to my thigh, I decided to run the risk of being called a rotten sport and eventually grabbed his jaws in my hands, pried him off, and handed him, spitting, hissing, and clawing, to his mistress.

As far as I can recall there was only one other evening of bloodletting on *Gazette*. It occurred during the height of the Hungarian Revolution, when hundreds of Hungarian refugees were being landed in Halifax. We had learned that among these people there happened to be a young man who was the Intercollegiate Fencing Champion of Hungary. We felt it would be interesting to bring him on *Gazette* and devote the evening to an interview on the subject of fencing. It took us only five minutes, after he arrived at the studios, to realize that we had a real prima donna on our hands. He was a haughty, demanding, and imperious young man whose sullen, scowling face spat out even the words "Good evening" as if they were an order. On the other hand, all of us connected with the program were simply dripping with charm and good-fellowship, grinning from ear to ear, offering him coffee and cigarettes so that he couldn't possibly mistake our little TV program for an MKVD interrogation.

The producer explained to him that I would question him about fencing, and that throughout the body of the interview he would have a chance to explain the various aspects of the sport. "After the interview portion is finished," the producer went on, "we would like to have you and Max stand up so that you can demonstrate on Max all the techniques you've been talking about. You'll each have an épée, and it should provide a nice, light ending to the program." But young Bela Lugosi was having none of this and chewed out the producer for offering up to him such an unworthy adversary on whom to demonstrate his skill. Finally the producer resorted to that old traditional North American argumentative technique, money. At the first mention of the ten-dollar honorarium connected with the interview, several centuries of fiercely passionate Magyar pride went out the window, and we had him in his studio chair within two minutes.

Toward the end of the interview, I got my one-minute signal, and after thanking the guest for a most enlightening dissertation on the art of fencing, suggested that perhaps he'd be good enough to give our viewing audience a demonstration of the various techniques and nuances of the art which he had just been explaining. Through clenched teeth he muttered petulantly that he would be delighted, and after handing me one of his épées, leaped like a gazelle out of his chair and into a most graceful fencing stance. I decided that my best defence would be to keep my épée slashing back and forth in front of me like a high speed windshield wiper, and this I proceeded to do. Actually, I had the blade moving so fast back and forth that the blur of after-images seemed like a metallic shield in front of me which I felt sure even tooth decay couldn't penetrate.

The first intimation I had that my oafish strategy wasn't working was when I looked down and noticed an ever-widening crimson stain spreading through the whiteness of my shirt just below my heart. At the time I was convinced he'd reamed out my aorta, but in true Errol Flynn tradition, I resolved to wait until the credit lines had finished rolling and the CBC cue had flashed on the screen before dying. It was a bit embarrassing when we were off the air, and a dozen big, strapping, hardbitten stage hands came rushing over to offer their services as seconds, to learn that it was a very superficial flesh wound. Moreover, it healed so rapidly that I was only able to enjoy for about a week the satisfaction of opening my shirt in darkened corners of the CBC TV building and proudly displaying my tiny Heidelberg duelling scar below my left teat to those male members of CBC staff of whom I felt reasonably sure.

My memories of those four years of wild interviews on *Gazette* have equipped me with some wonderful opening gambits or ice-breakers, which I still use and find most effective among the sophisticated and difficult-to-impress set of the Toronto cocktail milieu. One of my favourite throwaways is, "I'll never forget the evening Clement Atlee bit me!" While the eyebrows are still up under the hairline and the martini olive still teetering on the brink of the open mouth, it's best, if at all possible, to saunter off and become lost among the other guests before you can be pressed for details. At the risk of never again being able to use the line, I must divulge that the incident took place one evening in the *Gazette* studio when we had as guests three crew-members of a British submarine which was paying a courtesy call to Halifax. The lads brought in with them to the studio the sub's mascot—a dreadful, bad-tempered little spider monkey which, all through the interview, sat perched on my shoulder intently browsing through my hair.

I've always felt as confident about my personal hygiene as the next person, but whenever the camera dollied in for a close-up of the monkey, I could see on the studio monitor just off to one side that the little wretch was doing his best to give the impression that he was finding things—bringing the tiny pink fingers up to his beady eyes for close examination and then plunging them into my hair again for more imaginary goodies. To end the mounting and disconcerting embarrassment, I reached up in the middle of a question I was directing at the submariners and surreptitiously attempted to lift the monkey down onto my lap. Suddenly, I felt my index finger being encircled by his rotten little yellow teeth just over the knuckle and a slow, steadily increasing pressure being applied.

At the moment, one of the guests was explaining the difficulties of rescuing the doomed crews of submarines which fail to surface, and though I was beginning to feel nauseated from the pain, I felt it would be an inopportune moment to suddenly leap up and scream, "Aaaaahhhh!" all over the studio. I was able to take it for about another minute and then, convinced that my knuckle was going to crack in two, I very quietly and very formally interrupted the discussion of mass death beneath the waters by saying, "I'm awfully sorry, but if you don't get your monkey's teeth out of my shattered knuckle immediately, I'm afraid I'm going to be sick right here."

To his credit, the sailor jumped up instantly, in spite of the stunned look the non sequitur had occasioned, and made a grab for the monkey. The latter was so startled that it released my finger and leaped from my shoulder onto the camera. From there it jumped over onto the long boom from which the microphone was hanging and then over onto the curtains. The cameras then swung onto the monkey, and for the balance of the program the interview was forgotten as viewers were treated to ten minutes of the wildest acrobatics this side of the old Tarzan movies.

As it was now obvious that the monkey had completely taken over the show, I thought it might be nice to at least identify him for the viewers and so asked the submariners what his name was. At first they pretended they didn't hear me, and when I asked again, one of them, looking quite flustered, said, "We'd rovver not sigh, sir." It wasn't until we were off the air that I was able to corner them and ask why on earth they were making such a production out of not divulging the monkey's name on the air. "Well, sir," was the answer, "we didn't fink it would be quite proper. We calls eem . . . Clement Atlee!"

On one of my recent trips to Halifax, the CBC dug out of its TV film archives an interview on film which I'd almost forgotten. It was the one and only occasion when I was left absolutely speechless on *Gazette*. Always, no matter what went wrong, no matter what strange things the guests would come out with, no matter what havoc was wrought by animals, I would have recovered sufficiently by the end of the program to at least sign the program off in proper CBC fashion. This particular interview had taken place on the Common, a large, open stretch of grass in the city of Halifax where the Bill Lynch Travelling Show always set up shop when it was passing through. My task was to interview one of the carnival sideshow ladies named Consuela, who had an animal act.

Striving for a mood of relaxed informality, the producer had arranged Consuela and myself outstretched on the grass with her pet chimpanzee sitting between us. For fifteen minutes, Consuela answered all my questions concerning the animals in her life. She was very gypsy-looking and built like a brick cathedral. For the interview, she was wearing a brief, two-piece outfit, and during her long answers to my questions, I didn't quite know where to look. There was something morbidly fascinating about the way her bare midriff spilled down over her matador pants like a flesh-coloured truck tire. When I got my signal to wind up the interview I fell back on the old stock closing cliché, "This has been very interesting, Consuela, and now in closing could you tell us something of your future plans?"

At this point the camera began dollying in for a close-up of her, and just as they had her nicely crammed into the full frame she looked the lens straight in the eye and said, "Well, Mr. Ferguson, you might be interested to know that I'm expecting a baby elephant in nine months."

Since Halifax was a port city and very much navy-oriented, it was natural for us to decide one evening that we'd do a program on the subject of tattooing. I had been sent off the previous day to line up a tattoo artist who had set up his premises, with spider-like ingenuity, down near the waterfront, just about two pubs away from HMCS Stadacona. Sitting with me in his little back room,

he told me of the brisk business he did on naval paydays. With money in their pockets and two pubs to pass before they reached his tattoo parlour, a lot of ratings would stagger in and ask to have some large-busted mermaid inked into their fore-arm. He would make one fee out of this and then, invariably, a second fee a couple of days later when the same customer would return very sober and ask to have the mermaid converted into a rose, with the tender inscription "Mother". As we sat talking and I outlined generally what we would like him to do for us in the way of a television interview, I glanced around the little room and noticed that the walls were covered with panels of beaverboard, and that each panel was crammed with an infinite variety of tattoo designs, almost all of them dealing with either Mom, Dad, Sweetheart, or God. They were all his own creations, he told me, and by the time I'd examined them all and offered him a pleasant compliment on each one, I'd won his confidence and friendship for life.

"If you think they're something," he shouted gleefully, "wait till you see this!" He then raced to the walls, rubbing his hands like a character out of Dickens, and proceeded to lift off all the beaver-board panels. Underneath the panels and lining all four walls was a monumental compilation of glossy photos, none of which seemed to have even a remote connection with Mom, Dad, Sweetheart, or God. Terrified of being run in as a found-in before being able to complete my mission, I quickly arranged an assignation with him at our TV studios for the following day and beat a hasty retreat out into the fresh air of Hollis Street.

The next evening my little Marquis de Sade turned up at the studios and gave the viewers a dandy lecture on the history and techniques of tattooing. With about five minutes of program time left, he looked up from his array of needles, inks, and designs laid out on the studio table and asked would I like a demonstration. I told him I thought that was a capital idea and looked out expectantly at the dozen or more staging and technical crew standing with their big, brawny, virgin arms folded across their chests. When I asked for a volunteer, however, there was a great shaking of heads and sotto voce chorus of, "What the hell!"

My stomach sank when I heard my smart alec guest saying, "How about you, Max? You're not afraid of a little needle are you?"

Behind my sick TV smile of false bravado, I was furious with him for putting me on the spot before

thousands of Maritime viewers, and for a fleeting moment I toyed with the reprisal of telling all of them exactly what was behind all those beaverboard panels. I meekly extended a trembling white arm and stipulated that I wanted nothing more elaborate than just my two initials. Apart from a burning sensation, it was really quite painless and certainly nothing compared to Clement Atlee's teeth. As the Marquis traced out my initials, he kept up a running commentary on how the needle was penetrating at a speed of sixty times a second, how the ink was being imbedded under seven layers of skin, and how, consequently, I would carry this tattoo for life. The whole process took about thirty seconds, including the time he spent swabbing up the tiny globules of blood which oozed out along the needle's path.

After the program, while he was waiting in the TV lobby for his taxi, he thanked me profusely for the opportunity of coming on the program, and the last thing he said to me was, "You'll never know what this kind of publicity will do for me!"

Obviously, neither did he. Within a couple of months, he was behind bars at Dorchester Penitentiary doing seven years for trafficking in pornographic pictures.

For the next few days my arm throbbed and took on an angry red colouring from wrist to elbow. This, however didn't bother me half as much as the letter I received from a Surgeon-Commander in the R.C.N. in which he suggested I might like to read the paper he had just completed for the Canadian Navy showing the significant correlation between tattooing and venereal disease. I read it and hadn't felt so depressed since Uncle Tom's Cabin. However, within a week the arm was back to normal, and I was allowed to use the CBC bathroom facilities once again.

For sheer pandemonium, it was a guest with the mild and academic name of Professor Cato who gave me my worst moment on *Gazette*. When I had first heard the name, I envisioned a relaxed evening before the cameras, with some distinguished old Mr. Chips perhaps expounding on the use of the caesural pause in seventeenth-century French verse. However, I was soon to discover that there wasn't much of the academic about this Professor Cato. He was a 300-pound, seven-foot, professional wrestler from Japan, with one of the meanest faces you could ever hope to see. Though the war in the Pacific had been over for at least ten years I had the uneasy feeling that some blabbermouth had just told him the outcome. He wasn't the most talkative guest in the world, either, and after hearing all he had to say about his life story, his travels, his family, modern Japan, and his impressions of Canada, I realized only five minutes had been used up. In desperation I asked him if, like most professional wrestlers, he had a favourite wrestling hold. It turned out he had. It was called the Sleeper, and furthermore, he'd be willing to demonstrate it.

Having just become a father for the fourth time, I again looked out appealingly for volunteers among the dozens of strapping bodies lounging about the studio out of camera range. Again my invitation to instant stardom was greeted with most ungrateful and sullen mutterings of, "Are you kiddin'?", "In a pig's eye!", and various other forms of negation from the darkened depths of the studio.

Faced with the choice of filling with music for the rest of the interview or submitting to the experiment myself, I took the latter course, and within thirty seconds found myself standing in a judo costume with the giant immediately behind me. After hooking a monstrous arm around my neck from behind, he explained that the Sleeper Hold was really quite painless, and that I would feel no sensation at all before dropping off into the Land of Nod. The next thing I knew the arm had tightened like a python around my neck and I was fighting for breath. My head was throbbing, my lungs were burning, and I was sure my eyeballs were going to burst. It was without a doubt the most nightmarish sensation I've ever experienced. I can remember reaching up with both hands to try to pull the arm away from my neck, and my last conscious thought was that this was a psychopathic killer and, like a fool, I'd played right into his hands.

The next thing I remember seeing was a darkened studio with a blurred red light which I knew was the camera light. I was lying on the studio floor and I could hear the far-off murmur of voices I remembered clearly what had happened, but I couldn't understand why they had left me lying

there for two weeks. I was convinced at least two weeks had passed since I'd reached up to try and break that grip. Suddenly, light seemed to come flooding into the studio, and I saw Professor Cato standing over me. I realized then that I'd only been out for a minute or so, and apart from an attack of persistent coughing, I felt perfectly all right.

I thanked Professor Cato for strangling me and had just signed the program off when the control-room door flew open, and out rushed our producer, Bill Langstroth. Not the fun-loving, happy-go-lucky Bill Langstroth we currently see leading the Jubilee Singers, but a flushed and furious Bill Langstroth, who marched up to Professor Cato like the brave little tailor and ordered him out of the studio with the admonition that he was never to show his rotten face around those parts again. I was frankly embarrassed, and after the leviathan had skulked out I asked Bill why he had been so harsh on him. It was only then that I got the full story of what had happened.

After I had dropped to the floor, I immediately went into a convulsive spasm, and Maritime viewers, including my horrified wife and children watching at home, were treated to the fine, wholesome, dinnertime family fun of sitting through a series of my spasmodic twists and jerks, with my eyeballs rolled back into my head. Panic had set in immediately in the control room, and they punched up the *Gazette* title slide while filling in the background with neutral music—probably that grand old standby in moments of doom, Handel's *Largo*. My wife had tried to phone the studio to see what had happened, but the switchboard was jammed, and she had to content herself with rummaging through old insurance policies to see which were still in force.

It would be both an inaccuracy and an exaggeration to try to give the impression from all this that *Gazette* was unremittingly a program cut from the cloth of the old Laurel and Hardy comedies. There were many evenings when nothing at all went wrong, when all of us went about our jobs with quiet efficiency and brought off the program exactly the way the producer had originally intended. The Christmas Eve edition of *Gazette* in 1957 comes to mind in this category. Our producer had decided on that evening to forego our usual format and dispense with interviews. Instead, in an attempt to recreate for the viewers a nostalgic remembrance of an old fashioned Christmas, he had grouped the three of us—weatherman Rube Hornstein, announcer Don

Tremaine, and myself—around an open fireplace. There was to be, of course, a tinsel-draped tree, and toward the end of the half hour old Santa would appear with a real plum pudding, blazing merrily, which he would serve to us. We were then to invite old Santa to join us in the singing of *God Rest Ye*, and somewhere in the middle of this the program would fade out. It was the type of warm, relaxed program that needed practically no rehearsing. I think we spent a maximum of five minutes mapping out camera shots and making sure that the brandy on the plum pudding would light and keep burning while Santa carried it in.

During the hour dinner break before the actual show, I drove home in bubbling good humour, had a quick bite to eat, and started to head back down to the studios. As I walked across the lawn to the driveway I noticed my English bulldog, Toughy, sitting in the snow, shivering and looking like a forlorn and miserable Quasimodo. The poor, old grotesque head, creased and wrinkled and hanging in folds, was tilted up toward me with the two big fangs almost impaling the nostrils and the two pig-like, bloodshot eyes fixing me with the most appealing look. He may have the ugliest face in dogdom, but the bulldog is quite an actor. I was able to withstand only ten seconds of this Poor Little Match Girl routine before I opened the car door and invited him in.

When my producer met me walking in through the studio door with Toughy waddling behind me, he was a bit appalled. It was common knowledge around the studios that Toughy, ever since suffering a skull fracture, had become a bit queer in the head and was known as something of a troublemaker in the neighbourhood where I lived. Quite naturally, my producer's plans for rekindling in the minds of viewers some of the beauty and poignancy of Christmas that evening had not included the lumpish hulk of a mentally deranged and physically grotesque bulldog stretched out on the studio floor at my feet. To assuage his fears, I offered to push Toughy well under the chesterfield where, I assured him, the brute would not offend any sensitive eye and would sleep peacefully through earthquake, fire, or tidal wave.

And that's the way the program began—the cosy warmth of a grate-fire reflecting off the tinsel-drenched tree, the three of us relaxed on the chesterfield and through the haze of cigar smoke allowing "fond memory to bring the light of other days around us". As in most programs which are going well, the minutes raced by, and the sudden, bellowing "Oh, ho, ho!" of Santa, waiting in the wings with the plum pudding, came as a startling reminder that we were into the last minute. That same "Oh, ho, ho!" unfortunately penetrated the bedrock of Toughy's skull and impinged rudely on the pleasurable chimera of toads, slimy mud, and whatever other delights fill a bulldog's dreams on Christmas Eve.

Only after hearing the first explosive snort did I realize, too late, that the one thing Toughy couldn't tolerate in this world was a uniform of any kind. Out from under the chesterfield he came, in an obscene spread-eagle position because of the low clearance, but then after clawing madly to get traction he hurled himself at poor petrified Santa and engulfed at least two-thirds of the lovable old fellow's left buttock with his powerful jaws. Santa emitted a most heart-rending screech of pain and threw the plum pudding still blazing merrily, into the Christmas tree, which in turn quickly went up in flames. With the tree blazing, Toughy still hanging suspended by his teeth from Santa's buttock and the terrified face of Santa bequeathing a legacy of traumatic scars to thousands of Maritime children, none of us had the heart to sing *God Rest Ye* as planned and, instead, merely sat there, idiotically waving like stunned robots while the credit lines rolled down inexorably over Santa's agony, and the screen went mercifully at last to black.

from *And Now Here's Max*,
by Max Ferguson

Family Snapshots

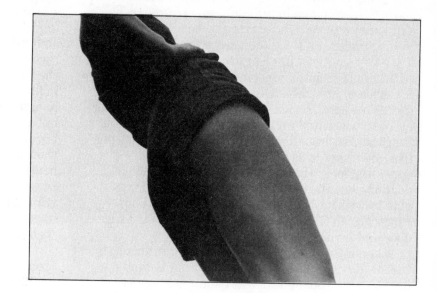

Pictures in an album
showing mountains
a partly naked girl
a family with too much blue sky
the car door ajar

Moments
captured imperfectly
by travellers and in-laws
who would not intrude
but who would have us know
where they have been
and how they have acted
in different places
in different years

They invite us
to turn the pages passively
and expect nothing
but the human scenery
of the wedding and the death
and pidgeontoed children
squinting before a camera
in the backyards of the world

There is no challenge
no denial among the pages
There are no newsclippings
of earthquakes or shootings
There are no photographs of accidents
no documents of divorce
no close-ups
Nothing really to leave behind

Nothing of who we are
or who the photographer was

Richard Hornsey

46

This is a Photograph of Me

It was taken some time ago.
At first it seems to be
a smeared
print: blurred lines and grey flecks
blended with the paper;

then, as you scan
it, you see in the left-hand corner
a thing that is like a branch: part of a tree
(balsam or spruce) emerging
and, to the right, halfway up
what ought to be a gentle
slope, a small frame house.

In the background there is a lake,
and beyond that, some low hills.

(The photograph was taken
the day after I drowned.

I am in the lake, in the centre
of the picture, just under the surface.

It is difficult to say where
precisely, or to say
how large or small I am:
the effect of the water
on light is a distortion

but if you look long enough,
eventually
you will be able to see me.)

Margaret Atwood

Me As My Grandmother

Sometimes
I look up quickly
and see for an instant
her face
in my mirror,
random tightness
turns my mouth
into a facsimile of hers,
eyes caught oddly
in the glass
make me
into her
looking at me.

Now that she's dead,
I understand
that it is right
that I should age
and wrinkle into her.
It brings her back,
it puts me into
the cycle of family.
We look at all time
with just that
one same face.

Rosemary Aubert

A little while and I will be gone from among you, whither I cannot tell. From nowhere we came, into nowhere we go. What is life? It is a flash of a firefly in the night. It is a breath of a buffalo in the winter time. It is as the little shadow that runs across the grass and loses itself in the sunset.

**Dying words of
Crowfoot, Blackfoot chief.**

Ham on Wheels

In real life she's a sweet, shy lady who works three days a week for a volunteer organization in a Toronto suburb, has two kids and a dentist husband and keeps a large home in meticulous order. At parties, aside from being prone to the odd attack of covert giggles, she's charming, retiring, genteel.

But when she steps into her little green Toyota and heads out onto the Don Valley Parkway on Monday, Wednesday and Friday mornings you can almost see her shoulders widen, her voice broaden and deepen, her expensive dress sag into denim coveralls. Her cigarette shifts from its prim position between her heart-shaped lips to the far left corner of her mouth, dropping carelessly. Her speech takes on a faintly southern drawl mixed with an odd Maritime inflection; her language switches from upper-middle-class English to an earthy street slang. Mrs. Carolynn Webster, like thousands of other car drivers on the highways of North America today, turns into a trucker every time she turns on her ignition. By the time she reaches the entrance ramp to Highway 401 you'd swear she was gumbooting a huge chuffing eighteen-wheeler down the six-lane expressway, shifting gears and hollering into her Citizen Band radio mike: "Breaker one-oh, break break!"

From somewhere out on the freeway an answer instantly crackles back: "Go ahead, break."

Mrs. Webster lets fly. "Hey hey hey, that's a big thanks for the comeback, good buddy! This be the one Lotsa Fun comin' at ya from old Toronto-town. A bright 'n glossy mornin' to ya, and what's your twenty come on?"

The answer booms back with an ear-splitting burst of static: "Mercy sakes there, Lotsa Fun; this be the one Leaky Tank from that Burlington-town; we be heading east on that four-nothin'-one, just past the Ajax turnoff for sure, go ahead."

Mrs. Webster looks cool. "Ten-four, good buddy, that puts you at my front door and on the lookout post. Been seein' any bears your end, come on?"

"Negatory, Lotsa Fun. I'd say you've got a clear shot all the way back to the Parkway ramp. I'll keep an eye on the door and let you know the score, go ahead."

Mrs. Webster looks pleased. "Hey, that's a big-four, Leaky Tank. I'll keep the back door closed for sure and raise you if they knock. Well, it's been great modulatin' with ya; just don't forget to keep that shiny side up and rubber side down, and take care cuz we care. Have a bunch of seventy-sevens and eighty-eights all over your cute little nose!"

She turns to me and grins. "It's great!" she says happily, hooking the microphone back into its holder. "I've even stopped kicking my cats."

The Citizen Band (CB) radio fad is without question an astonishing phenomenon. It is proving to be, at the very least, one of the hottest fads ever to hit the North American gadget market; CB radio sets are even outselling stereos and the redoubtable television set. In less than two years, CB radio has burgeoned into an industry worth thirty million dollars annually in Canada alone; the American figure hovers around two and a half billion dollars. Over seventeen million sets are already on the air throughout North America, two million of them in Canada, and the number is growing at the rate of well over half a million *per month*.

In Canada, the department of transport is reeling under the unexpected onslaught of license applications. It has virtually given up trying to go after the estimated thirty percent of CB buyers who fail to register their sets. "I mean, just how much point is there in trying to catch a berserk elephant by the tail?" a harassed transport department desk clerk asked me, rolling his eyes toward the ceiling. "We're having enough trouble trying to get this operation expanded and computerized so that we can handle the stampede of people who bother to stop and pick up a license."

Actually, CB radio (or General Radio Services [GRS], as the department of transport insists) isn't as new a phenomenon as it may seem. In Canada, the eleven-metre band, once used by ham radio operators, was set aside for cheap civilian communications as far back as 1962, but CB sets in those days were expensive, complicated units, full of tubes and so bulky that most of the set had to be installed in the trunk of the car so as not to interfere with the driver's movements. As a result, not much interest was shown by the civilian population for GRS, and for the next dozen years the number of licenses issued never exceeded about 100,000.

Then, in 1974, the Arab oil embargo hit the North American driver right between his gas pumps. Gas and diesel fuel was in short supply all over the world and many American states and Canadian provinces scrambled to reduce highway speed limits to fifty-five mph to decrease at least some of this continent's enormous fuel consumption. For those of us who drove ordinary four-wheelers (cars, vans and pickup trucks), this new limit was an irritant but hardly a hardship.

For the drivers of trucks (eighteen-wheelers), however, it was a disaster. In practical terms it meant fewer runs and less pay, which equaled more problems paying off truck mortgages, which spelled potential bankruptcy.

The truckers were furious but, since many police forces were enforcing the new limit with considerable enthusiasm, they had little choice but to slow down. Paying for a lot of "green stamps" (the fines levied for speeding) was just as bad as losing pay, with the additional possibility of loss of license.

By happy coincidence, CB radios had by this time progressed to the printed circuit and transistor stage, which made them smaller, cheaper, more dependable and much easier to install. The truckers figured that even if only one out of every four of them installed a CB set in his cab, they'd have themselves, almost overnight, an electronic grapevine that would rival the communications system of a nation-wide telephone company.

The rest, as they say, is history. In less than two years, two out of every three trucks on North America's highways had their "set of ears." They could provide each other with advance warning about police and radar traps as they revved their huge rigs back up to the seventy mph to which they'd become accustomed. As a handy spin-off, the constant exchange of weather information and road reports made a long-range trucker's life a lot safer, and the chance to "ratchet-jaw" (talk) with other truckers during the long nights on the highway made it less boring. All in all, the idea was a winner.

And that's where time should have stood still, in the opinion of many disgruntled truckers. They remember those days with a certain fondness, days when the air waves were mostly open and you could talk sensibly to other sensible human beings, most of whom also happened to drive trucks. But times change: I remember turning on my regular AM car radio one night early last summer and listening with bemusement to a strange but catchy country-and-western song which kept mentioning "smokeys" and "rubber ducks" and something about "banging the hammer down" and "catching you on the flip-flop." Hundreds of thousands of listeners must have scratched their heads over the meaning of that song, but by the end of the summer everyone had found out and the craze was on. Song after song rolled off the hit parade romanticizing the trucker as a lovable sort of bandit who talked racy jargon and seemed to spend most of his time in the big rigs, playing hide-and-seek with the highway patrol.

This was a myth that one could climb into. Inside the safety and comfort of one's own car one could become *involved*. For just $150 and an aerial, through the magic of transistors and printed circuitry, one could relate almost intimately to a family of hundreds, even thousands, of "good buddies" out there, all busily separating themselves from each other with more and more electronic gadgetry in a desperate attempt to get together.

Less than a year later, the highways are crawling forests of antennae and the air waves chatter with fake truckers talking fake truckers' talk to other fake truckers, straining to lay an eyeball on one of them thar smokeys at the front door, requesting weighty weather information about stretches of highway so close ahead that the recipients are often driving over them as they receive the reports. Impromptu caravans are created on the spur of the moment, and "the front door and back door" (the first and last car in the line) keep watch for anything of interest and report whatever they see to the rest of the convoy, which can, in the meantime, rest easy. Instant aerial friendships spring up and last anywhere from several seconds to several hours, as long as the parties involved are traveling within radio range.

Better even than that, CB radio also provides an irresistible escape from everyday reality by allowing a CBer to assume virtually any identity he or she likes. All the characteristics or physical handicaps which in real life might be a disadvantage are irrelevant on the air, and so they disappear. It's a documented fact that stutterers often manage virtuoso performances on CB, and normally shy people often lose their customary reticence and hoot and holler like the life of the party.

The word performance is the key word here: it doesn't take more than a few hours of monitoring the CB air waves to realize that CB talk has precious little to do with communication in the usual sense. What it's all about is ritual, a string of little one- or two-minute performances in which jargon is mixed and matched in snappy-sounding combinations, and the longer you can keep it going, the more impressed your audience is. The number of CBers anxiously waiting in the wings to jump in and do their shtick is so great that conversations are rarely allowed to continue beyond a minute or so before the next performer calls for his "break."

Performances or not, most CB conversations, or "relationships," manage to maintain some reality, unless the CBer gets carried away and makes the mistake of trying to carry them over into the real world—which means anywhere outside his or her car. Robbie Smith (The Bookie from Kitchener-town), a young woman who sells books for the McClelland & Stewart publishing company and is an avid CBer, told me a very typical tale about a trip she'd taken through the American midwest. She stumbled across another CBer on the open road where the air waves were less cluttered and longer conversation was possible and, after talking to each other for many hours, comparing impressions of the scenery and describing other places they'd visited in their lives, they decided to pull into a truck stop for a cup of coffee.

"It was the weirdest thing," she remembered. "Here we'd been talking to each other for hours like old friends, really opening up to each other, and yet when we met at the restaurant door and sat down across from each other over that cup of coffee, we couldn't think of a thing to say. Not a single thing."

She told me that story while we were driving up to Sarnia, Ontario, to sell the local library some books. A little later, she became involved in a conversation with a trucker who was on the road a couple of miles behind us, traveling in the same direction. For my benefit, she developed the conversation over twenty minutes or so, then grinned at me sheepishly as if to say, "All right,

A Glossary

At my front door—Ahead of me
Ban a U-ee—Make a U-turn
Banging the hammer down—Pushing down on the gas pedal
Bear in the air—Police aircraft
Bears—Police
Big-four—Same as ten-four
Blew my doors off—Passed me rapidly
Break or *Breaker*—Request to communicate
Brown paper bag—Unmarked police car
Brush your teeth and comb your hair—Warning: radar ahead
Bubble trouble—Flat tire
Bucket mouth—Excessive talker
Chicken coop—Highway weigh station
Clear shot—Police-free road
Comeback—Response
Copy the mail—Listen to the CB talk
Doin' the double nickel—Driving at fifty-five mph
Draggin' wagon—Tow truck
Dummy loads—People who babble to no purpose
Got your ears on?—CB turned on?
Haircut palace—Overpass or bridge with limited clearing
Hamburger Helper—Illegal amplifier used to boost the power of a set beyond the legal limit
Handle—A catchy name used for identification

Holding on to your mud flaps—Following closely
Hole in the wall—Tunnel
I'll keep the back door closed—I'll keep my eyes open for any police coming up behind me
Keep your ears clean—Keep your equipment functioning
Kojak with a Kodak—Police with radar
Modulating—Talking via CB radio
On the flip-flop—On the return trip
Raise you—Call you
Ratchet-jaw—Talk
Seventy-threes—Best regards
Seventy-sevens and seventy-eights—Love and kisses
Shiny side up and rubber side down—Drive carefully; don't flip your car
Sitting down by the side of one-oh—Listening but not talking on Channel Ten
Ten-four—Message received; OK
Ten-ten—Message completed
The big switch-on—Keep your equipment turned on
Smokeys—Police
Walking the dog—Occupying the channels
What's your twenty?—What's your location?

you watch," and asked the trucker if he'd like to stop for coffee with the two of us. He said he would, and we agreed on a truck stop dead ahead.

We were already in the café and watching out the front window when an enormous cattle trailer pulled off the highway and into the parking area, air brakes hissing and the great diesel revving noisily between gears. A short, thin man jumped out of the cab and pushed through the café door, grinning nervously. He looked us over and we looked him over, and then we all studied the menu with grim determination. I was quite taken aback; on the radio, he'd sounded bigger and certainly more self-assured. Eventually Robbie made a few remarks and then I said a few things, but he was extremely fidgety and kept misunderstanding what I was saying. I finally had to admit there was no contact at all. We'd just been disembodied voices on the highway, playing an intriguing little game with an electronic toy, and now we couldn't fit the people to the voices. Less than ten minutes after he'd come in, the trucker got up and left, having suddenly remembered an urgent deadline. "You see," Robbie shrugged, "That's invariably how it is. Nobody looks like they sound, because everybody sounds like who they want to be, not like who they really are."

While CB radio is reviled by some as another in the series of electronic alienation devices with which we're going to do ourselves in one of these days, it does offer some direct benefits. In the United States many state patrols have outfitted their policemen with CB radios, and they report an impressive increase in the speed with which they've been able to respond to automobile accidents, general misadventures, and even crimes. In Canada, the Ontario Provincial Police recently established an experimental four-station network along one of the busiest 100-mile sections of Highway 401, at London, Woodstock, Kitchener and Milton, to test the usefulness of direct CB contact with the public. Signs have been mounted at regular intervals along the highway, announcing to drivers that the OPP is monitoring Channel Nine, the emergency channel. If the program is successful, the provincial police are prepared to add a whole string of base stations over the 500-mile stretch of Highway 401.

Meanwhile, CB clubs have been springing up all over the country. Some of them are little more than hobby clubs which sponsor the odd "jamboree" (picnic) or "coffee break" (evening get-together), but many of them actively train CB neophytes in the practice and ethics of proper radio communication. As well, they make their more seasoned members (plus equipment) available to local police forces for search and rescue operations. Initially delighted with such generous offers, the police have since sobered a little and now tend to screen out all but the obviously bush-wise volunteers. A few hair-raising experiences with groups of CB-happy amateurs falling merrily over cliffs and into ravines in a mad hunt for a lost child, who soon became virtually a side issue in the desperate attempt to get all the "rescuers" home alive, have given police cause for caution. Nevertheless, in the hands of mature searchers, intelligently organized and linked by CB, these radios and their operators can make the difference between success and failure, life and death. In outlying areas, where telephones are scarce or even nonexistent, they can be even more valuable.

The CB clubs have also been linked with the annual brouhaha known as Halloween. CB clubs now regularly form a CB-linked "Halloween patrol" in many Canadian communities on Halloween night. Some patrols, in fact, like the idea so much that when Halloween ended they decided not to disband, and now conduct regular evening patrols throughout their neighbourhoods. I must admit that the idea rendered me a trifle thoughtful, but both the police officers I queried seemed to see no harm in it. "Well sure, I suppose any community's going to have its share of frustrated would-be cops," one agreed, "but I don't think that necessarily leads to vigilante-type antics. If it does, you can be sure we'll crack down on it."

I'm sure those officers meant just what they said, but they obviously hadn't heard some of the wilder stories which have been coming out of the Ottawa area lately. One club became so overwhelmed by what it apparently saw as its divine calling to rescue and save that it outfitted its members with old World War II gas masks and cheap first-aid kits, as well as a police siren for one of its members and an illegal "cherry" (flashing red light) for another. One man boasted that, upon hearing of an accident on his CB, he jumped a highway median and sped to the accident scene *up an oncoming highway lane, against traffic.* "Well, no," the president of this CB club was quoted as saying to a reporter from the Ottawa *Citizen,* "we never took any St. John Ambulance course or first aid because, if they don't want us the way we are, to hell with them!"

There is virtually no such thing as a casual CBer.

The minute someone puts a CB set into his or her vehicle, that person becomes a CB fanatic. It's like a virus against which there is no known cure. Once infected, a CBer tends to embrace the cause with such passion that the club "coffee breaks" I attended almost always sounded like pell-mell barroom brawls. CBers argue over issues such as "clean air" (trying to stop obscenities on the air waves), jammed channels (overfull radio airspace), the proliferation of bad radio manners (hogging air time, abusing the use of emergency channels), and on and on. In Texas recently, one man's temper flared when another used abusive language on the air; the two argued about it heatedly, then finally decided to fight it out under an overpass. They had no sooner begun to fight when a third CBer, furious at them for sullying the air waves, arrived at the scene, pulled out a pistol and shot them both.

On the more humorous side, prostitutes have recently begun to use CB to solicit business from all the "truckers" on the highways. Maverick preachers advertise their spiritual wares on CB channels and in the more rural areas, where the air waves are less congested, would-be disc jockeys broadcast whole mini-shows. Parents have begun to use CB as a handy way to by-pass the baby sitter, going off to parties or the movies with walkie-talkies tuned to a channel preset on another set in their homes. The hassles that start when the kids begin broadcasting nonsense in all directions from the base station have almost brought some CBers to blows or into the courts.

An increasing number of motels along well-traveled truckers' routes now accept reservations via CB radio. Some will even hook a CBer into a regular telephone line for local calls to wife or business. Many farmers' wives use CB to call their husbands in from the fields when dinner is hot, and an increasing number of bored housewives and househusbands use CB base stations in their homes to talk to anybody at all who will listen.

With all that action on the air waves, CB channels get very little rest and, as a result, CB radio airspace around most of the larger North American cities is now crowded almost beyond belief. It's at the point where even Channel Nine, the emergency channel, is sometimes used by irresponsible CBers to prattle away, potentially blocking out calls for help and real emergency announcements. Some fully accredited CB emergency monitoring organizations have actually given up in disgust, closing down many of their big urban operations "because it's pointless trying to hear anybody through all that bull." And many veteran CBers automatically turn off their sets when they come within thirty miles of large cities.

Fortunately, some badly needed help is just around the corner. In a desperate effort to alleviate

the jam-ups, the US Federal Communications Commission, the Canadian transport department and the communications ministries of various Central and South American countries recently put their heads together and hammered out a cooperative plan to add seventeen new channels to the current twenty-three, giving us a grand total of forty. Reciprocal agreements which will permit Canadian and American tourists to use their sets when driving on the other side of the border are also in the final stages of completion. In Canada, the new forty-channel sets go on sale this month and become legally usable on April 1 [1977]. In Mexico, CBers can throw their sets away. After monitoring the CB air waves in their own country and then listening to descriptions of the future complexities of such a communications system, Mexican government officials threw up their hands and scrapped the whole affair.

I asked John deMarcado, director general of the Telecommunications Regulatory Service of the department of transport, if Canadian officials have been tempted to do the same thing. "Oh no, certainly not," he assured me. "Yes, I admit that things are a bit hectic at the moment, but this will all settle down eventually. We're already looking at ways to double and even treble the number of GRS channels to alleviate crowding, and there will be a lot of refinements to the sets which will make them far more useful and sophisticated than they are right now. Despite all the abuses going on at the moment, I still think that GRS is a great idea."

And so, no doubt, do CBers Russ and Dora Starret of Red Wing, Ontario, whose recent family tragedy served to demonstrate the positive side of the CB phenomenon in a rather unusual way. The couple and their five children were left destitute when their home burned to the ground on the morning of March 5, 1976. Within minutes of the disaster, CB air waves throughout the area were buzzing; CBers from miles around joined an operation headed by Grant Edwards, president of a Collingwood GRS club, to help the Starrets. Furniture, appliances, clothing, food and cash poured in from all directions, and by nightfall arrangements had even been made for a temporary home.

"You see, that's what I mean," a Collingwood acquaintance who listened in on that operation said to me. "Sometimes I get the feeling that the air waves are just full of dummy loads and bucket mouths walking their dogs, but when you see an operation like that coming through, you get to figuring maybe this town *is* big enough for all of us. I get pretty groused up about all this CB baloney sometimes but when you get right down to the old nitty gritty, radio people are pretty good eggs, most of 'em."

Andreas Schroeder, *Weekend*

Tee Vee Man

William E. Baldwin, technician, sat cross-legged on his bunk, doggedly chewing the end of a pencil. Wedged between his knees was a clipboard holding a paper covered with neat columns of figures. A passing crewman might have supposed that he was working out the formula for a world-shaking discovery. "Two hundred," he muttered. "Two hundred and two, specifically, for roofing and chimney repairs, paint, and new fencing. Dammit, even on risk pay we never get ahead."

As he looked away from the unchanging figures, Baldwin glanced at the bulkhead beside him. A trio of smiling faces looked back at him, seeming full of pride for their spaceman hero. "Hero," he bit out grimly. Little did his wife and children know of his true position on the space platform. With sudden bitterness, Baldwin slammed the clipboard into his tiny locker and stretched out tensely, hands behind his head. On this unique platform, this little flyspeck, were thirty-five of the best brains that Earth had produced. Thirty-five genii, gathered from nearly as many countries—and Baldwin, employee of International Communications: Baldwin, the Tee Vee man. His mouth tightened as he sub-voiced the words.

Tee Vee man. It didn't seem to matter that only three of the twenty-seven satellites he serviced were television relays, that the rest were vital navigation, weather, and surveillance satellites. To the indifferent thinking-machines around him he was the TV technician, a target for superior smiles, a body grudgingly given much-needed space, food, and air. These men, designers of most of their own jealously-guarded equipment, would have thrown a fit if a mere engineer so much as peeped into their private work areas, much less traced a circuit. He was unwanted there, and virtually ignored elsewhere when he chanced on conversations involving anything from space medicine to astrophysics. Perhaps it might have been different if he had gone on past his Master's, put off marriage a little longer, even turned down the job offered to him by the hybrid giant that had eventually sent him out here.

The glory of research and design had worn off when he found that international politics could reach into the depths of his lab, but he had not learned the full lesson. It had remained for him to be wooed into space training, to arrive on the space-platform and find himself considered hired help. Only then could he realize that he was caught between two worlds: in the one a professional who knew too little of business and politics, in the other a hireling of business and politics who knew too little of the professions surrounding him. In neither world, it seemed, was he judged as an individual, by merits that had weight in normal situations.

"At any rate," he growled, "in two months my tour is over. One more after that, and back to solid ground for good. But not back to I.C. Back to school." On that thought, and the probability that he would have to move his family again, Baldwin reached for the clipboard, hoping to work a little magic on the cold figures.

"Baldwin . . . Baldwin . . . Communications."

He dropped into the narrow aisle, stepped to the hatch, lifted a phone and thumbed a button. "Communications . . . Baldwin."

"A wee job for you, Tee Vee," said the dry voice of MacPherson, mathematician. "One of your yo-yos, TV 2, is out of service. Terrible fuss from downstairs, and you're to get on it, as of now. I've run a tape into your bronco, and you've five minutes minus twenty to most favourable position. You go down the North Pole chute this time, and just so you won't buzz your old folks in Canada I've plotted the whole course. Don't get lost, man, the set in the lounge is actin' up."

"Right," snapped Baldwin, and moved off through the passage toward the Hub and the airlock. He cursed mildly to himself. It would have to be a TV satellite. Probably it had been Melling who sent the message. To him everything was an emergency, since he was obviously uncertain of his future in the company. A holdover from the original, he was in danger of replacement by Zoldovski, his counterpart in the "other" original, and half the time his budget was held up by the Red Asia bloc.

Reaching the airlock, Baldwin suited up, then dropped the air pressure and checked out. Everything working fine, as usual, he thought, and as he flexed the pliothene gloves he added aloud,

"Probably still too much heat dissipation." Well, he'd had a touch of frostbite every time out. He pumped the remaining air back into the tanks, opened the outer hatch, and dove across to the bronco. He slipped the single mooring cable and closed the hatch, then settled into the huge seat and hooked up his suit connections. "Communications . . . Baldwin. Radio check."

"Five by five," answered MacPherson. "Your red light shows in ninety-three minutes thirty, so you've not much time to do the job. Up at the South Pole, laddie, and don't be late, as we've a one-shot sighting to take. Besides, your Mister Melling says it's vital to have the African network back in the grid within two hours. Twenty-two seconds, Baldwin. Don't catch cold out there."

Baldwin fumed as the webbing closed around him. The Scotsman seemed to be rubbing it in, as usual. He could just as well have homed on TV 2 and not taken any more time, once he got below the Van Allen Belt. Then, suddenly, he was shoved back into the seat as the bronco took off at maximum gees. For a wild second he considered strangling the Scotsman. "Full acceleration, and then full deceleration," he groaned. A very poor joke, or a nasty way to show him his place. Whichever it was, he would have a talk with MacPherson when he got back. Then, as acceleration lifted, he turned to the job ahead.

MacPherson had mentioned the African network—it would have to be that area to cause such a furor. If only the satellites had come a little later the dark continent might have had cable or microwave connections to the world grid, to serve in just such emergencies as this. Then there wouldn't be a scream of anguish every time some South African housewife missed The Internation Cookbook. As the bronco's verniers spat briefly, bringing it under the Belt and down in a sweeping arc across Labrador and Newfoundland, Baldwin twisted and looked up at Earth, to spot the dawn band lying full across the eastern Atlantic. New curses rattled behind his teeth as he estimated it to be about 10 a.m., in Algiers. Then his head snapped forward as deceleration began, and his temper neared the boiling point.

Below TV 2, at a remote spot in Central Africa, the capital city of a small, newly-independent country was nearing its boiling point too. A mass of contradictions, the city of some fifty thousand was a place where anything might happen, and something quite ugly could happen on this particular day. Anyone approaching Ungalah on the ground, along every road including that from the country's one airport, would have been struck by large groups of semi-permanent huts, each housing a few members of a different tribe. Their pointed roofs echoed the lines of a single, great ultra-modern building soaring above and beyond them, at the centre of the city.

At the edge of the city proper wretched, ramshackle quarters of all descriptions huddled and leaned against one another, giving way only a few streets from the huge central square to old shops, then modern, spacious stores. Late-model vehicles mingled with wood-burning buses and oxcarts; neat-suited businessmen and government officials with tribesmen in local costume. Normally the babble, screech and clamour would have been deafening, but today there was an uneasy quiet over most of the city. Only in the square facing the government building was there any sound, any real sense of life. Here four thousand tribesmen from the northern province sat, squatted, and stood, body to body, murmuring among themselves, gesturing toward the end of the square. The assortment of arms among them, carried in open defiance of the law, was antique by modern standards, but nonetheless deadly. That these men and their weapons were a force to be reckoned with could be judged by the numbers of nervous troops ranked in front of the great building, ranged down its flanks, and scattered through the lobbies.

It was neither the tribesmen not the troops facing them, however, that commanded immediate attention at the moment. Rather, it was a strange device raised precisely at the top of the broad steps leading up to the buildings. Fully twenty feet high and thirty long, it had a vast hood extending out from its top and down its sides. Even as the tribesmen were becoming dangerously restive there came a crackling, a sudden whine which slowly died away, and a figure appeared on what now could be identified as a TV extension screen.

As the screen brightened, this figure became recognizable, and though none of them had ever been in to the building behind the screen it was obvious to the watchers that he was seated in a room somewhere in that building. A bellow of disapproval rose, and one giant of a man, clad in little more than a massive headdress, waved an ancient sword as he pushed toward the screen through the milling mob. Then as the figure spoke the din slowly settled into silence.

"My friends from the north," the seated man said in grave tones, "it would give me great pleasure to welcome you to the capitol on any occasion, if you had come in peace. Indeed, although I am leader of the opposition party, and the prime minister is of your venerable tribe, you have been most hospitable to me on my visits to your villages. Your response to me when I have spoken to you on the great picture makers in your own province has always been courteous too, so I am told, though you seem not to choose my vote tokens at elections."

Here he smiled tensely, and a wave of ironic comment swept the square. At the far end an old, bent and scarred veteran shouted a rude suggestion about the tokens and the young men gathered around him, lifted him high in the air so he could repeat it. In his office on the top floor, the seated man turned from the cameras and stole a glance out the window at his side, down into the square, to see a ripple of movement spread from the old man like waves from a dropped pebble. He wiped his palms on his trousers, under the desk, and continued.

"I can understand your mood today. You want to see your leader. There are certain people who would like you to think that he is in some sort of danger. They have told you that he has come to harm, that we of the opposition have taken him away, that we have dealt with him as other leaders, in other times, have been dealt with." A hint of revulsion passed across his face briefly, as below the giant waved his sword again and screamed at the screen, drawing a hideous response from the tribesmen behind him. "First let me say," the voice boomed over them, "that those times are gone. As many things have passed away and new things have taken their places in our lives, so new ideas have come to us, new ways of handling the problems of leadership, new ways of settling differences of opinion. I, Albert N'Galy, swear to you that your leader is safe."

In the pause that followed, men looked to the old veteran, now standing on a stone bench, and to the giant, who suddenly found himself almost under the screen, yards in front of the rest. The old man, conscious of his growing power, once again hurled abuse down the square toward the distant screen, while the giant, uncomfortably close to the troops, turned and voiced his rage to the crowd in incoherent shouts, punctuated by thrusts of his sword.

One, two, five minutes went by as the tumult reached its climax and subsided, while in his office the speaker waited and watched, sweat soaking into his shirt and jacket. Choosing his time carefully, he spoke forcefully but without shouting into his microphone, overriding the dying roar.

"Your leader is safe. I repeat. Although he is many miles away, across the sea, Nicolas N'Thulmah is quite safe. Indeed, he is acting for all of us to receive an honour which we must find almost impossible to conceive. At this very moment he is in the company of the head men of all the great countries of the world: he, our leader, is to speak before them, to carry our thanks for being welcomed into the great assembly of chiefs, United Nations. It is a time of which we should all be proud, not a time to behave like animals."

In the square, the giant was silent as he tried to digest and assess this new information. Behind him muttering began, swelling slowly into a roar, and the old man cried, "It's a trick. Show us N'Thulmah. Show us Nicolas the Beloved."

The figure on the screen stood up, held out its hands. One more time, desperately aware of the scene below him, N'Galy was able to subdue the mob. "Many of you have seen on the picture makers people moving within United Nations on important occasions. It has been arranged that we should see Nicolas N'Thulmah welcomed, as our leader, to the great hall of chiefs. If you see him there, will you believe he is all right?"

The old man pondered this for a moment, as a small buzz of consultations went round and slowly grew into a confused sound of assent. Sensing the mood of those around him, the old man held his silence, content to wait for the right time. The figure on the screen sat down again, and his face grew until it filled the screen. The onlookers could see lines of strain, the look of anxiety, as he stared straight out into the mob.

"Then you must be patient a little longer," he said. "It is only a matter of a little time. There are some problems with the picture maker's workers. They cannot make the picture come across the ocean yet. But it will not be long." His voice increased in volume toward the end of this statement, as he anticipated the reaction below, and it was immediate in coming.

The giant was shouting again, moving toward the base of the screen, and the tribesmen surged toward him. At the rear, the veteran began a chant and his young followers joined him, spreading it until the whole far end of the square resounded with the one word: "Now . . . Now!" On the top floor, N'Galy nodded toward his office door and an officer moved to the elevator. Below him, harried non-coms moved back and forth, out of sight, cautioning, checking, encouraging their men as the sounds of frustration and disapproval rolled over them.

Frustration and disapproval were still with William Baldwin too, as the bronco homed in on TV 2 and automatically matched course and velocity, with a precision that worked to less than one kph and a thousandth of a degree. He turned on his floods and watched as the turning satellite seemed to move in and up on his starboard side, an inch at a time, until it blocked out the blackness of space. At last all relative movement ceased. He saw the last green light come on, turned his suit on to self-function and disengaged it, locked the propulsion panel, and extended his work shield in a semi-circle around TV 2. One more careful check of the control panels and he climbed out the hatch and along the flooring of his shield.

A fantastic amount of knowledge, some of it gained from painful experience, had gone into the design of this part of the bronco. Here, mounted or stowed in the shield itself, were tools, meters, spare gates and rods, an auxiliary control panel, the visuo-library index for securing all information concerning the satellites under his care. Some things he had installed himself, just as a large amount of the design in the satellites had been modified, on his insistence, to facilitate maintenance aloft. In the old days, before the platform, a satellite had either worked or been replaced, but when it became economical to service them in orbit, sweeping changes had occurred. Even when Baldwin had no inkling that he would become an early "repairman" he had put nearly all of his time into standardization of design and simplification of access. It had already paid off a thousandfold.

TV 2, antennae automatically retracted by gyroscopic equipment apparently still functioning perfectly, turned on its axis with a deceptively lazy motion that was still too fast for a visual check. Baldwin carefully extended booms, snapped them to the eyebolts mounted on the satellite's axis, and fastened his lifeline. Diving out to the end of one boom, he snapped a switch in the eyebolt and kicked off back to the shield. He brought slight pressure onto the booms and watched the great satellite slow to a stop, moving it in close with the damaged area facing him. Something had holed the skin, peeling it back over a two-foot gash between the points of entry and exit.

He glanced at a meter in the shield, knowing that it would show a reduced internal temperature, but though it was dropping visually, it was still not as bad as he had expected. Working sunside would make it easier anyway, he thought, and started the

Jesperson equalizer. Heat bathed the area as the collectors on the front of his shield began to function and the dissipators spread it around TV 2.

He pulled a cutting torch from its holder and methodically cut away the jagged pieces of fuselage, placing them on the flooring where they clung lightly. This was the simplest part of the job, and as he worked he allowed his mind to return to MacPherson and his colleagues. He knew that none of them realized how intricate or dangerous this work could be. The library was a cute gadget, but actually the technician relied mainly on a crammed memory, ingenuity, and sometimes inspiration. There simply wasn't enough time to do much rehashing at orbit, and if he did pull one and haul it back he had lots of time for review at the platform, though he'd have to sabotage his radio to keep off the abuse from below.

The impact area was cleared now, and he turned back to the job at hand, checking the large chronometer face near the top of the work shield. Twenty-eight minutes to red light. He concentrated on the satellite. "Number three power supply, all units," he grunted, as he pried at the fused mass. It had thrown a little radiation around too, but not into any vital sections. He flexed his suit gloves thoughtfully and dug deeper into the guts of the satellite. Have to swing one gate at least, he mused, and reached for the magnakey. With both feet planted, and one hand on the satellite, he placed the key over a slug with great precision. Pressing the stud, he activated the magnet and felt the slug move up and out. A half-turn locked it in the out position and he moved to the next.

Six slugs later he was looking at the rest of the damage. Two rods of video useless, all of the power supply, a section of hi-voltage cable, and probably one more rod, to be sure. Quickly, almost mechanically, he extracted the wrecked components, not bothering to replace anything individual. Like pulling hen's teeth, he winced, as tiny prongs twisted and broke in their sockets and he went after them one by one. He took two adjacent rods as an added precaution and spares for these went into place easily. Eighteen minutes to red light.

He wired in the hi-voltage-cable with a spot welder. Next the video units went in. One of them went hard, but he got it into place and it checked out. Last the power supply had to be eased in. He even smiled slightly as he hefted the one hundred odd pounds of ultra-light miracle, thinking of what a job it would have been to handle it on earth. All

connectors in place, he moved to his bank of meters and remote adjustment equipment. Fingers moving quickly, he set dials, snapped switches, watched a tiny monitoring screen. The antennae slid partway out, just clearing the shield. Power on. A high reading in the video stages . . . damped. On the screen a blurred scene began to appear. He made more adjustments from the panel, and noted the results as they were completed within the satellite. The picture was clearing. Too late he realized that TV 2 was swinging in behind him, that the booms had somehow become unlocked.

As he reached wildly for the boom controls, the bulk of the satellite touched his leg, pressing it against the pile of fuselage fragments. Pain shot through his body, blinding him, threatening to black him out, and then it was over. The huge mass swung slowly, idly backward. It had been a light brush, not enough to crush his leg, but it had been enough. Fighting off terror, he looked down at his suit. Only a thin line appeared to tell him that a fragment had sliced through the self-sealing unit, and his dial told him that there was no leak. But inside the suit something far more serious had happened. He could feel a jet of warm fluid splashing against his leg, feel the warmth of his own blood seeping down around his ankle, into the boot of the suit. Panic rose in him again as he knew that an artery was severed in the calf of his leg.

Struggling to remain calm he dove across the flooring and whipped out a piece of spare cable. In near hysteria he wrapped it tightly around his leg, a little below the knee. He fumbled with it, managed a clumsy knot, stuck a screwdriver through it, and twisted. The pain became intense, but he felt the pulsing jet slow and seem to stop. No time to judge whether it would hold against suit pressure, or what it would do to air circulation. He shot a glance at the chronometer as he cleared the shield flooring and flipped off switches. Seven minutes to red light.

He grabbed a large piece of patch metal, much too large for the job, but there was no time to cut it now. The satellite was too far out now. Swing the booms—lock them this time. Working frantically he tacked corners and ran a rough weld down the edges. No time to make a further check, no time to lock the gate, the welded section would have to hold it. Dizziness was mounting in him as he moved hand-over-hand to the end of the boom and snapped the eyebolt switch. He dove back to the shield as TV 2 began to spin again. Hit the boom release, climb back through the hatch. As he passed the monitoring screen he could see a black

figure, mouth working silently. His last thought as he fell into the seat and wiped his hand across the propulsion panel and shield retractor switches was that he had never checked the audio. Then, as the red light went on and webbing closed around him, acceleration crushed him back into the seat and on into oblivion.

In the city of Ungalah, bolts snicked back on weapons as the troops straightened their ranks to face four thousand surging tribesmen. Far down the square, the old man, carried on eager young shoulders, urged the crowd to vengeance, and at the very top of the steps the giant, all feelings banished now save the lust of battle, waved his sword and screamed a war cry. Muzzles came up as the mob hit the first step behind him, heads turned slightly toward officers whose arms were upraised to give the signal. Then, suddenly, a new cry rose in the square.

From back to front it swept the ranks of tribesmen and all movement stopped. Every eye turned toward the screen as the face of Nicolas N'Thulmah swam up out of greyness. The view changed slightly and behind him the background of the United Nations Assembly Hall appeared. Abruptly the liquid, smooth voice of their leader filled the air. His language was strange, but it was clearly his voice. Then it was replaced by one speaking in their own tongue, their own dialect.

"Many of you here," it said, "have become accustomed to the welcoming of a new nation to your ranks. A few, more recent members, will understand, will recall, the emotions that fill me as I accept, for my people, a place among the nations of the world."

The rest was lost as a thunder of triumph rattled the windows of the government building, and swords and spears waved a fierce greeting to the leader. The sound seemed almost to shake Albert N'Galy down further into his seat, but as he tilted back his head and closed his eyes he smiled weakly.

Back aboard the space platform, William Baldwin reclined, if one could call it that, in the narrow confines of his bunk. He grimaced distastefully at the bottle hanging from the bunk close above his head, and the tube leading to his arm. Slowly, painfully, he raised himself slightly and looked down the length of his body. His blanket was pinned securely. Well, he thought, doctors are the same anywhere, whether they're space researchers or horse doctors. From the feel of it they put ten pounds of dressing on my leg. I'd probably be better off with a horse doctor or a good G.P.

He settled back again and wondered what would happen now. Would they send up a special replacement for him? Melling would have a fit if that were necessary . . . it would take pretty near the whole U.N. portion of the budget for a year to do that. But then, he mused, someone will have to go under and finish the job on TV 2: it can't be a first-class performer with that patchwork. But why should it be Baldwin who risked his neck again, why shouldn't it be some other sucker sent up to take over this thankless grind, someone with a thicker skin? Then, despite himself, he grinned. That could be taken as a rotten pun. He winced with pain again as he turned on his side to see who had come through the hatch, and felt a stirring of the anger as MacPherson came alongside his bunk.

"Well," frowned the balding Scotsman, "loading on the company's time I see, eh Baldwin?" The injured man felt his face flush, and he pushed up slightly to throw a hot reply back, but the Scotsman went blithely on. "I've a wee communication from your Mister Melling for a change. He says you're to take as long as you need to recover, but he would like you to touch up TV 2 in a couple of days. Seems it's a mite wobbly on its axis, and the audio fades."

Baldwin fell back on to his pillow. No reprieve, he thought. I should tell him to go to . . .

"Oh yes," continued MacPherson, "there was somethin' else too." He glanced at a flimsy in one hand. "The U.N. sends its appreciation for your prompt action during crisis. You, uh, removed the possibility of a bloody insurrection in some unpronounceable African state or other." He rolled the words with an exaggerated burr, and for the first time that Baldwin could remember the dour Scotsman smiled. "And we thought the occasion demanded some little token, since you won't be able to go down in person for some time yet. This is from all of us." His face grew serious again as he brought his other hand from behind his back. Between thumb and forefinger dangled a ribbon, obviously cut from someone's underwear, and and from it was suspended a gigantic, star-shaped piece of metal. Scratched into it in bold letters was the word, "Hero".

MacPherson turned to leave. "The butcher-boys say you can hobble in three days, and get back to work in a week, but they're like all the male midwives down below. Just between us, can you kind of rush it? The set in the lounge is gettin' really bad now, and we need a Tee Vee man." He popped back through the hatch, whistling, as Baldwin lay back and held up his medal.

H.A. Hargreaves

Violence, Envy, Rage

There seems to be little argument over the fact that violence plays a major part in the public story-telling—movies, television, books, plays—of this historic period. The following notes attempt to explore some of the sources of that preoccupation with violence, and some of the explanations given for it. But before discussing that, I want to describe the community to which that fictional violence is offered, the community that pays money for it, accepts it, and apparently enjoys it. And here I proceed without documentation or footnotes, intuition being my only guide.

My experience, as writer, husband, father, citizen, teaches me that I live in a community—I'm speaking here of North America and the democracies of Western Europe—which is dominated by envy. Most of the people around me, no matter how successful they may be, no matter how much they may have exceeded the original goals of their adult life, are profoundly envious of one another. This envy is without question a part of the human condition but in my view it is heavily reinforced, and distorted out of all proportion, by the mass media and the messages they deliver to us. We—the last few generations or so, but especially the generation that came to maturity in the television age—have to contend with something none of our ancestors faced: we feel compelled to watch, every day of our lives, an unending spectacle of riches displayed before us on the screens in our living rooms and (to a lesser extent) in our cinemas. The pictures on these screens describe to us a life that in many ways seems superior to the one we lead. That pictured life is glamorous, exciting, sexually fulfilling, lacking in drudgery or boredom. It is lived by persons who are more handsome than we are, and apparently more satisfied with their work and their private lives. Most of these persons—whether they are in spy stories or situation comedies or sports programs—seem to move effortlessly from one absorbing event to another. Naturally, they arouse our envy. At the same time, while these programs seem to stimulate our envy *accidentally*, the commercials which interrupt them do so *on purpose*. The commercials describe to us a life that is better than the one we live—full of comradeship, love, glamour. This is the life we can have, the commercials imply, if only we purchase the products named. We know that it is a lie, yet we are unable to restrain the feeling that somehow we have been cheated of something. The effect of television, I am trying to say, is to make us unhappy with what we have or may ever hope to have—and I believe this is a more important effect of television than the violence it may or may not cause.

The result of this much envy can only be a permanent, barely suppressed (and not always suppressed) rage. We grow angry at what we lack; and, as the year of television-watching constantly reminds us of the inadequacy of our lives, we grow angrier still. But television and movies offer us an antidote. They sell us a cure for the disease they have helped produce: violence. They offer us a temporary release in the form of horrendously violent movies and programs that release—for only a moment, of course—our worst angers. As I've said elsewhere, this is a solution, of sorts, in the sense that heroin is a solution to an unhappy family life.

Robert Fulford, from a report to Ontario's *Royal Commission on Violence in the Communications Industry*

Ontario Secondary School Students Discuss 1867 in 1967

"I think Confederation is a good thing."
"I think it is a bad thing. I'm against it."
"I'm for it."
"What good will it do you?"
"What harm will it do you?"
"No harm, I just don't like it."
"Well, I do."
"Let's have a vote."

From *Translations from the English,*
by J. R. Colombo.

Next To Nothing At All

What's going on?

A question that many people are asking these days but one more easily asked than answered.

In an effort to find out what's going on I eavesdropped on two persons in a restaurant yesterday.

Talking to a friend from around the bay was a resident of the city:

"What's going on out your way? Anything . . . or what?"

"Nothing, boy, nothing."

"Nothing at all, eh?"

"No, nothing at all. Well, no. Not nothing at all but next to nothing at all. What's going on in here. Anything at all?"

"Nothing, boy. Well, little or nothing. Let's put it this way . . . there is and there isn't."

"Not much going on anywhere, seems like. Well, I suppose there is a bit going on here and there but nothing here. Nothing at all."

So it seems that what's going on is nothing at all. Or very little. Hardly enough, apparently, to keep the mind alive.

Ray Guy

I only wish that you could come back when you're my age to see the kind of Canada that you'll see. So dream your dreams, keep them and pursue them
—John Diefenbaker

Political Speech

This pearl of political oratory was almost lost to history. It was recorded by a CBC newsman at a nominating convention before the 1974 Ontario provincial election, but never played on the news because its special qualities could not be handled within the traditional news format. So Ken McCreath, the reporter who'd gone out to cover the event, brought the tape to As It Happens, where we aired it. We felt that it belonged to all Canadians, not just the lucky few who happened to attend the local meeting.

May I suggest that you read the speech aloud in order to appreciate its charm. The tone you want on this is cheerful bombast. I'm afraid that some opening phrases are missing. It took the reporter a moment or two to collect his wits and start recording.

Our anonymous MPP, by the way, was returned to office at the next Ontario election. The Miss Morrison whom he was there to introduce has not been heard of since. I wonder if she's still even a Tory—imagine having to follow this remarkable address.

"Either we have a thing we believe in or we don't. And if they don't, then get them out. But I happen to believe in those kind of people who believe in the kind of people you are. And I kind of believe that this is the place that I can make the kind of speech that I want to. And if you don't want to make that speech, well, that's fine and dandy.

"Oh, you can talk about it. Oh, yes sir, you can talk about *it*. We can talk about it from over here and we can talk about it from over there. And we talk—but don't you come back to me, or to the people that succeed me a hundred years from now, and say you didn't believe it. Because we're going to come back and we're going to say we rammed it down your throat. And that's the way it's going to be."

[*A gentle nudge here from the Chairman to get on with Miss Morrison's nomination.*]

"Yes. And I know we only have four minutes and I'm going to say something. Because, deep down, you know what we are talking about and beyond that you know what we're *really* talking about. And, you see, we're running out of time. And we're running out of this and we're running out of that.

"I'm going to say to you something. That about a year from now you're going to talk about Miss Morrison and about the things she said. But the one thing that I would like you to remember is that regardless of what is said about Miss Morrison, or about this or about that, is that it really fundamentally comes down to the right time to sing. And therefore I am turning over to you, Miss Morrison.

"Thank you."

from *As It Happened*, by Barbara Frum

A Note on the Public Transportation System

It's not hard to begin
a conversation with the person
who happens to be seated
nearest you, especially when she's been
reading with apparent interest
a book that's one of your
favourites and can't find
her matches.
      The difficulty is
once you've spoken you can never
go back to being comfortable
with silence,
      even if you learn
you've nothing to say
and would rather not listen.
      You can stop talking
but you can't forget
the broken wires
dangling there between you.
      You'll smile almost guiltily
when your glances
accidentally bump.
      It may get so bad
that one of you will have to
pretend to fall asleep.

Alden Nowlan

Hat

i lost my hat on the subway
when i realised i'd left it on the seat
they closed up the doors
having blown the whistle once more
shortly thereafter i stood out in the street.

i went down to the lost and the found
but all that they'd had turned in
was a revolving gargantuan facsimile
that just sat in the corner & grinned.

so as not to go home empty handed
i claimed that it was mine
and the man wrapped it up
and he gave it to me
saying "many people misplace this kind . . ."

now there it sits on the mantelpiece
and i show it to all of my friends
some say, "gee, that's real nice!"
others are non-plussed
but I know that it's . . . THE END

Joe Hall

Everybody Knows But Me

You told Bobby's girl Betty
Betty told Bobby last night
Bobby told Eddy
at the A & W
And Eddy told Freddy and Dwight
Dwight went and told his girl friends
And the fool has two or three
And they spread the news through the whole dang to
So everybody knows but me
    I'm a fool
Everybody knows but me

Morris told Ellis and Osgoode
And they're on the football team
In a matter of minutes in the cheerleaders' mood
They thought that it was really a scream
And they're playing lots of away games
And they tell everyone they see
How I am your personal private fool
So everybody knows but me
    I'm a fool
Everybody knows but me

Jesse Winchester, from his record, *Let the Rough Side Drag*

Women

The party was finishing and Valentine was happy. The man she found so attractive seemed to be attracted to her too. All evening she had felt him watching her, felt him as though he had been caressing her, and her skin was aflame from his insistent gaze.

Like any woman who senses she is being observed by a man who pleases her, she found it difficult to remain natural and had to take care not to speak and and laugh too loud. Also she occasionally had to tear herself away from the group he was in and rather held it against him that he didn't follow her when her duties as hostess took her into the big room.

She was happy and exhausted. That constraint that a woman feels not to take the first step when what she wants is to hover round a man, as girls simply do so simply with the boys they take a fancy to, that denial left her sorely tried in every muscle. She was almost relieved when he came to say goodbye.

She was smiling a little foolishly from the effort it cost her to hide her joy, because he had just said, "If you're free one night this week and if you'd like to, I'll come and take you out to dinner, and afterwards we'll go dancing," when her friend Mariette passed by and called, "Can I use your telephone to call a taxi?"

Why in the world are we always so anxious to rob fate of his role? He would work things out perfectly well himself without our pushing him on and always chiming in when it's not our turn to speak. Valentine said, "Just a minute, dear," and then, "Would you mind taking Mariette, André?" And that was it!

The two of them got into the long car with its chrome grill, its "thousand-dollar smile" gleaming gently in the night like a luminous trap. At once André began speaking enthusiastically about Valentine, of her grace, her charm, her figure. Mariette listened in silence.

"Well, don't you agree?"

"Of course I agree! No one knows Valentine's qualities better than I do. I've known her for fifteen years. You were talking about her nice figure. I wish she could hear you, she'd be pleased. She had to work so hard to lose all that excess weight she put on during her marriage."

"Weight? You're joking. She's as thin as a string."

"Exactly. Just the way she was before she got married. You know how it is. When you've won a husband you sometimes forget how it was you won him. You get a bit slack. When Valentine became a widow of course she wasn't exactly what you'd call obese, but—I often tell her, 'If you can't marry without getting fat, better forget it.' She's really ravishing now, isn't she?"

"Absolutely."

"Same thing for her hair. You didn't know her before she began to dye it?"

"No. I thought she was naturally auburn. What colour was her hair before?"

"Well as a matter of fact she was auburn before too. But during the last years of her marriage she turned quite grey. It's only since she became a widow that she changed the colour. It's so much more becoming. She looks fifteen years younger than she really is. If Daniel could see her he wouldn't recognize her."

"Did you know her husband?"

"Oh, very well . . . the poor thing."

"Yes, indeed, to die so young."

"It's not so much that. I don't think Daniel was all that interested in life. He seemed so relieved to be leaving it that it was quite depressing, I must say."

"Really? Didn't they get along together?"

"Not very well. And yet of all the men I know Daniel had nearly every imaginable quality."

"Sometimes it's just a question of irreducible incompatibility. After all, Valentine has fine qualities too."

"Of course. For that matter they were a very happy couple to begin with. It was only when Daniel began to have business difficulties that things started to go wrong."

"Yes, well, a run of bad luck can make a man bitter and impossible to live with."

"And women too. But what can you expect, it's human nature. Valentine was used to a certain luxury. I thought, like everyone else, that they had married for love and that a little adversity wouldn't change a thing. They even say that a loving couple is brought closer together by tribulations. I know for my part that if I were married and my husband happened to lose his fortune I'd say to myself, here's a chance to show him just how much I love him. It would take more than that to make my hair turn grey. But Valentine is a spoilt child. At the beginning of this setback word was going around that she was, how shall I say it, trying to make up for what Daniel could no longer give her by—by—"

"By having a rich friend? Is that what you're getting at?"

"Well, yes. That's it. But I never believed that."

"At any rate those were the days when she was still fairly slim and fairly auburn."

"Don't be mean. I hate that. She doesn't deserve it. She just lacked a little courage. That's no crime."

"Just the same, the life she's living today must require a lot of courage. She works very hard."

"But then she earns a lot. You must do the one if you want the other. When she married Daniel she thought her future was sure forever. It was a bad gamble. Oh, I'm not worried about her. As she has often said, the next time she'll choose a man of more substance."

"Really? She says that?"

"Well, put yourself in her place. You can't understand that, can you, a man who's shovelling money all day long? I can't understand her either. But my trouble is that I'm sentimental."

"Money doesn't interest you?"

"Me? You don't know me, do you? A warm heart and a humble cottage, as they say, is all I need. And I could even do without the cottage."

"That's great. And have you found them?"

"No. Because in other respects I'm very demanding."

"For example?"

"Intelligence. I could only love a man who was extremely intelligent."

"Next?"

"And had excellent manners. I can't stand boors."

"Is that all?"

"He must be physically attractive. Don't laugh, it's one of my weaknesses."

"Well—those standards would make the vainest of suitors tremble."

"You're a fine one to talk. You meet them all easily."

"Does that mean that I stand a hope?"

"What are you getting at there? Don't think I've forgotten Valentine, and I can assure you she's got all it takes to make such a thing out of the question. Friendship is something I respect more than anything in the world."

"Well said! But what if I told you that Valentine means nothing to me. Nothing at all, I swear it. If you're free one night this week and if you'd like to, I'll come and take you out to dinner and afterwards we'll go dancing."

Six months later, on his way to lunch, André ran into Valentine. He asked her to join him.

"You look very happy, Valentine."

"I should hope so. You see, I'm getting married."

"Ah! Do I know him?"

"Not likely! He's not a banker, he's a painter."

"A well known one?"

"Well known? No! He's a poor devil who's full of talent but completely unknown."

"Really?"

"What's the matter? You look quite surprised."

"I am a little. You'll think me crude asking this but—when a person marries an unknown artist, how do they live?"

"From hand to mouth. And then, I'll go on working. I don't mind. No, I never take breath, thanks."

"Afraid of getting fat?"

"It scares me skinny. You know, my first husband had the tastes of a Turk. He liked his women round. Protest as I might I was never plump enough. Afterwards I had a terrible time getting back to my old shape."

"Didn't you want to stay the way he liked you?"

"That would have seemed pretty unhealthy to me. As they say, one must live with the living."

"You must have resented his peculiar tastes."

"Daniel's? The poor dear, I'd have done anything for him."

"Did you get along well together?"

"I would even say we were scandalously in love with each other. Even though I'm marrying again I'll always cherish my memory of him. I know I made him happy. I don't feel any remorse."

"Are you sure you made him happy? It seems to me that's very difficult to know."

Valentine fished around in her handbag and drew out a small card that she passed over to André. It was one of those cards you find in florists' shops. Daniel had written: 'You've made me the happiest of men!'

"That was the card that came with the last flowers he sent me. I'll never part with it. It may seem a little stereotyped as a declaration but just think, he was going to die, and he knew it. What a wonderful man he was!"

"You really loved him that much?"

"Yes. When I knew that he was condemned my hair turned white in a few months. He didn't want me to dye it because it had turned white for him. He had become a little childish as many sick people do."

"Come on, now. Don't be too sad. Tell me, you weren't too annoyed with me for not telephoning?"

"A little, yes. I can tell you now that at one time I had almost begun to fall in love with you. I was just waiting for a little encouragement. It didn't come. I was hurt, I must admit. But since you preferred Mariette—by the way, how are you two getting along? I never see her any more. When are you going to take the step like my painter and me?"

"Mariette? Hmm. I think everything's over with Mariette."

"Well, that's news. Since when?"

"Why, since today. You see she only likes men who are extremely intelligent."

Claire Martin, from *Avec ou sans amour*, translated by Philip Stratford.

Housewife

I never thought I'd feel like this
At my age. I thought by this time I'd be
calm and serene,
Occupied by things like gourmet recipes
And refinishing old tables.

Instead of that it's like seventeen again,
March flashes through my flesh as it did then,
Leaving me weak and warm and wondering
What happens next? Will people think I'm strange
With my hair long and straight, though streaking grey?

Why can't I reconcile myself to proper dresses
And hairdos more becoming to my age?
My mother did, and lived in peace
Or did she? I can't believe she ever felt
As I do now, but how would I know, really?

My daughters think I'm sensible and solid,
Someone who's always there, to call them in the morning,
To cook the roast, and order pants from Eaton's;
What would they say, I wonder, if I told them
I'd like to go play marbles in the mud?

Or waltz around the kitchen while a country singer
Warbles about falling to pieces; is that what I'm doing?
I never was much of a dancer, although
I always wanted to be. Maybe that
Or something else is what's wrong with me now.

Helen Porter

On the Road to LaScie

Ahead of me and to the left
I see a twisted figure
dancing in the dust
and when the swirling brown cloud
scatters in the air about his head
I see it is a man
an old man making fists
with one hand and hurling them
like a punch-drunk prize-fighter
at a truck disappearing now
over the next hill

with his other hand
he is waving me down
and I pull over to see what's the matter
not because I'm naturally kind
to strangers on the road
but because there is something
frantic something of an emergency
in his wild and dusty dance

I have visions of his wife or son
or someone lying in the ditch
bleeding and broken
a hit and run case I think
wondering how I'll handle it
knowing well my mind's weakness
for the sight of blood

there's been no accident however
no hit and run no body in the ditch
all he wants is a lift
to the next village
his widowed sister called
and asked him to come down
to cut some firewood for her
she has five kids but none
old or strong enough to cut wood

her husband drowned last spring
when he ran his boat up on White Sail Rock
coming in from the island
one night blind drunk
so now she's left alone
with her kids and no one
to cut firewood
so twice a week he goes down there
to help her out

curses her dead husband
every step of the way
slays him again
with every swing of the ax

Al Pittman

Dancing

Long ago
when I first danced
I danced
holding her
back and arm
making her move
as I moved

she was best
when she was
least herself
lost herself

Now I dance
seeing her
dance away from
me
      she
looks at me
dancing
        we
are closer
held in the movement of the dance

I no longer dance
with myself

we are two
not one

the dance
is one

F. R. Scott

Dancer with Bruised Knees

(When I first knew her
she was a dancer
She would leap confidently
Knowing that should she fall
It would be into the arms
of her very own partner
She never failed
to get a curtain call)

For years we had been one with the stars
A pas de deux of renown
I'd leap and he'd catch me on the fly
And gently he'd put me down

The heights that I reached were dangerous
And I saw my partner strain
And felt when I had landed
His strength was on the wane

Back before my knees were blue
Backs broke bending in a step for two

For years we had been one with the stars
A pas de deux of renown
I'd leap and he'd catch me on the fly
But once I came crashing down

Now I'm a weaver
Wall hangings if you please
In every one I feature
A dancer with bruised knees

For years we had been one with the stars
A pas de deux of renown
I'd leave and he'd catch me on the fly
But once I came crashing down

Anna McGarrigle, from the record, *Dancer with Bruised Knees*

Youth and Bliss

It didn't take the bliss moguls long to discover the potential in the North American youth market. Maharaj Ji (who, after all, is just a kid himself), the Reverend Sun Myung Moon, and L. Ron Hubbard have made a fortune selling a sense of purpose and a reason to get up in the morning to middle-class kids who don't know what to do with their expendable dollars and their expendable lives. What the gurus market is joy. For that, they demand something that purchasers don't value anyway, control of their lives.

When she was sixteen, Linda Epstein bought Hare Krishna. For three years she happily hit the pavement on Yonge Street in Toronto every day, begging-cup in hand, blissfully content to be a cipher in a sari. Linda collected money for a destination she didn't know or question. Like Scientology, the Divine Light Mission, or the brand of Christianity marketed by that Mao in a business suit, Sun Myung Moon, Hare Krishna works by keeping its followers ignorant of everything except the movement's particular brand of truth.

Linda Epstein was as unremarkable as all the other devotees and might have remained so, except for the fact that her father decided to tussle for her mind and hired Lightning Ted Patrick to restore her to her senses. Thanks to the cults, Patrick has his own little industry going, selling his de-programming services to hurt and angry parents who can't bear the embarrassing defection of their rebellious offspring. Patrick works on the theory that the cultists are brainwashed victims of sinister masterminds, victims who will only be saved when the trance is forcibly broken. It's a pleasing explanation, no doubt, to parents who don't understand how their children could knowingly reject them.

When Ted Patrick was finished de-programming Linda, a press conference was called to celebrate the family's reunion—as though the parents thought that some publicity would vindicate their pain and solidify their victory over Hare Krishna.

It didn't work. In a matter of weeks, Linda was back downtown at the temple. I've talked to her twice on *As It Happens*, once while she was grateful for being rescued from the cult and later when she was grateful to be back. On the first occasion, the "retrieved soul" sounded rather frantic. Her answers came back at me so fast and so jumbled that she was almost unintelligible.

Barbara: Are you Linda?

Linda: Yes, I'm Linda, and I'd like to make a few points at the beginning. I'm not going back to the temple, whatever means they try. We only got like one meal a day and slept four hours. And we were working, selling books very hard on the street like for about six hours, seven hours, eight hours a day. It wasn't out of my own free will but because the pull of the hypnosis was so strong. I collected like maybe a hundred dollars a day on the street. I was so tired. I was really overworked. Sometimes I'd fall asleep on the street. And I'm really glad to be back because like I was just completely overworked.

Barbara: What kept you then? Why didn't you walk out the door?

Linda: I was under the hypnosis and total brainwashing. I was afraid, psychologically afraid to leave, because if I left I would have nowhere to go because my mind was attracted to the chanting and I just had nowhere to go. My mind was programmed to think that I should just keep chanting and thinking I was doing the work for God.

Barbara: Can you tell us how you were programmed?

Linda: Through continuous chanting of the Hare Krishna mantra, like four hours in the morning, four hours in the evening, classes, scriptures, chanting, and they make you think that you're working for God and that everything should be given up for God. So they have people sent out on the streets to take money from people and—

Barbara: But Linda, if you were so overworked and underfed, what kept you there? Do you remember wanting to get away and not being able to?

Linda: It's like when anyone's hypnotized, you're in a trance. Like I thought I was giving up for God. I was programmed to think that. We have no choice. Psychologically, we were afraid to leave. Sometimes people leave on their own, but they have nowhere to go. They just don't know where they're going to work. They just don't fit into society. So Ted Patrick, he's the de-programmer, he takes people out by permission of their parents and he tells you the evils of the cult. There's different cults. There's five hundred of them. And he tells you how you're being tricked, how you're being used as a prostitute.

Barbara: That's what Ted Patrick said?

Linda: He says that to everyone. He says the same amount of words to everyone during the de-programming.

The next time I saw Linda was in the studio

several months later, right after she went back to Hare Krishna—just as giddy, just as frenzied, just as convinced now that she was right in rejecting her father and Ted Patrick—but clearly a lot more contented.

Barbara: Why did you go back, Linda?
Linda: Why? Because I was pulled out against my own will and I had a repressed desire in me to go back all the time, but my father said that if I went back he'd personally grab me and then they'd have the de-programmers for four months and they'd keep me in a room. I was really scared because I was really confused. They were shooting down everything I've ever done and they were blaspheming our movement and our spiritual

master and I was just so scared, I didn't know what to do. I'd see the devotees downtown. I'd talk to them. How can you ignore them? I've known them for years. They're my friends and the only people I really care for. I just want to know God and this is my way of doing it, you know. My father is an atheist and if he doesn't want to do it, it's fine with me.
Barbara: What do you mean by saying that the devotees are the only people in the world you care about? Your father and mother cared enough to want to save you from making a terrible mistake and from being controlled.
Linda: I'm not controlled. I can come and go freely and see my parents if I want. No one forced me to come back. I came back on my own. Like when they pulled me out, they gave me a list of things to say and my father said he'd beat the hell out of me if I didn't say them.
Barbara: We talked to you then, too, and you were just as convinced that Hare Krishna had brainwashed you. Which is it? Which is really you?
Linda: See, the thing is, like Ted Patrick has a philosophy—this brainwashing philosophy—that people are hypnotized and this and that. I never heard about that until he started talking to me. And like he completely breaks your resistance down. I didn't know what to think and I started accepting what he was thinking because that's the only thing that I kept hearing over and over again and I was just so scared.
Barbara: Yet when you were describing the de-programming, you said you were scared at first, but then you realized that Ted Patrick cared about you and about helping you.
Linda: But every day I could tell that I was missing them. I would talk about the devotees and Krishna and the temple and I kept thinking about going back, but I didn't have enough courage, because I was threatened that if I went back—like there's a Hell's Angel who's a de-programmer and I didn't want to do that whole thing again, that whole torture thing, with all this yelling and screaming and Bible verses and all these things. Like, I'm not kidding, they'd make a list of things I'd have to say and if I didn't say them, my father said they'd beat the hell out of me.
Barbara: What's the state of relations between you and your parents? Are you going to be able to talk to them ever again?
Linda: I hope so. They don't really want to talk to me. I called them twice in the last two months.
Barbara: What did they say?
Linda: "We don't want to talk to you or have

anything to do with you. Don't bother us. Why don't you just come home?"

Barbara: Do you feel for them at all?

Linda: Yeah, because they don't try to understand. They can't live my life forever, you know.

Barbara: What do you think brought you back to the temple?

Linda: Chanting Hare Krishna and the devotees. The girls there that I knew.

Barbara: Is it a special caring that you got from them?

Linda: Well, yeah, we're all endeavouring to become God-conscious, to become Krishna-conscious together.

Barbara: Then again, your parents also love you. They gave birth to you and reared you.

Linda: Yeah, but we try to not be attached. I was never really getting love. I never really was close to them, anyways. I don't miss them now or anything. I never missed them before, either. I call them every now and then and just keep a distant relationship. A lot of people do that because there's nothing there. Like, I thought maybe if I went back to school and contacted old friends, I'd be happy, but I wasn't happy. I just kept getting back to Krishna-conscious activities. So the proof is there. Like, I wasn't really de-programmed—whatever that means. It's obvious that my father didn't get his money's worth.

Barbara: What do you see ahead for Linda Epstein?

Linda: Becoming God-conscious. Like, I've always been interested in finding out about God. I'm here and I enjoy what I'm doing—telling people about Krishna and selling books and things. You know.

From *As It Happened*,
by Barbara Frum

Poet Cop

As Hans Jewinski stands at the lectern and recites his poems to the students at Scarborough College I can't help but think that some day on a Toronto street this big, moon-faced man will lean out of a yellow cruiser and tell me to pull over. He'll be all business then, not this hulking panda bear who's telling the students what it's like to be a cop on duty at the Santa Claus parade.

> they wouldn't detail me
> to the santa claus parade
> last year a father complained
> when i answered his 8 year old
> that i wouldn't have been there
> if there weren't a santa clause

The students love it. Jewinski wears a dark blue pullover and faded blue, flared trousers with mud caked at the cuffs. His bulbous rubber boots anchor him to the floor like two tugboats. He wears a "Cops are tops" button on his shirt.

Jewinski, thirty, has been writing poetry since he was a high school student in Scarborough, or "Scarberia," as he calls the place. He joined the Toronto police force in 1971 and has gained a considerable local reputation as a poet cop, which is the name of a paperback book of poetry which he had published in 1975, and which has sold 30,000 copies.

The police force doesn't object to Jewinski's readings, even though it often means a frantic rush in his red Volkswagen to get to work at 4 p.m. at Fifty-one Division, even though it means television and radio appearances and having his picture taken in uniform. "I get some good-natured ribbing from the guys," he explained, "but the force has really been nice. I guess they figure it's good publicity."

His parents didn't want young Hans to be either a poet or a cop. They wanted him to be a doctor or a lawyer. His brother went to work in a factory, after all, and so all the pressure was on Hans to make a career as a professional. He studied at Waterloo University and during one year he hitchhiked across Canada and the United States, lived on a commune in Ohio for four months, and kept sending his professor letters explaining why his essays were late.

He decided to be a policeman after spending a day in court, ostensibly to observe the lawyers in action as part of a career-planning day. He emerged more impressed with the policemen he watched in court. "They were the only ones who seemed to know what they were doing," he said.

Of course, being a cop also provides rich material for a poet. He's guarded the Rolling Stones from hungry groupies. He's given mouth-to-mouth resuscitation to corpses. He's been on duty at noisy demonstrations at the United States Embassy. He's been to robberies, drownings, domestic disputes, tavern brawls. He knows hookers and winos. He once chased two thieves who made off with a pink flamingo at Riverdale Zoo and when he found them they already had broken the flamingo's neck and were cooking it over an open fire. They asked if he'd like to join them, and he did, or at least he says so in a poem called, When it's too late, it's too late.

> . . . when would
> i ever get a chance
> to eat cabbagetown-fried-flamingo?

Jewinski's poetry has appeared in the Canadian Forum, The Fiddlehead, Old Nun Magazine, Ward Seven News, and Tamarack Review (and a handful of such obscure publications as Missing Link Magazine, Queen Stree T Magazine, Invisible City, Gut, and Impulse). He has published a booklet of poetry, Poet Cop Two, that measures an inch by two inches, with type so small you have to squint to read it.

He takes notes on the run. The worst place to jot down ideas or compose is on duty in "the yellow car." The police radio keeps squawking to life and he admits he'd look silly if something important came over and he was in the midst of creation. He finds days at court, waiting in the corridors for his cases, excellent times to compose.

Life for Jewinski is one paradox after another. When he was a "typical long-haired, bearded, hippie freak," he got cracked over the head by a truncheon-wielding cop in Chicago. Later, as a Toronto policeman, he worked at the Amchitka demonstration on University Avenue and encountered a young woman who had helped him in Chicago. "How could you?" she said when she recognized him, armed and in uniform.

And there was the time at the police station when he was getting a coffee for a young radical brought in for questioning. When his back was turned, the young man pushed all Jewinski's notes in a pile on a table and set fire to them.

> Why i ask
> abbie hoffman said
> "destroy the pig's communications"
> so i did
> as i take him back to his cell
> he asks me about his phone call
> "excommunicated" i say
> and go back to my table to rewrite
> the poems he burned up

Martin O'Malley, in The Globe and Mail

Tracks

he told her it was like nothing she had ever felt before
he told her everybody was using it
he told her there was nothing to be afraid of
he told her nobody would know
he told her they would look like freckles anyway
he told her everything would be all right
he told her
and he told her
and he told her they were broke
and he told her nothing else would ease the pain
and he told her how to earn the money
and he told her nobody would know
and he told her everything would be all right
and you tell me that she/d been a mixed-up kid
and you tell me that you/d known right from the start
and you tell me that you/re clean
and you show me your smooth arms
and you tell me i/ve got nothing on you
and you tell me everybody knows
and you tell me everything will be all right
and i tell you you had better make tracks
or i/ll kill you

Hans Jewinski

Do the Panthers
Play the Blues for Stephanie

the harley is
painted silver
and the red saddle
is studded with
chrome tacks

it carries a
california license
plate and a red
and white flag

his afro
is bleached
and the tattoos
on his arms
and hands are
day-glo red

on the street
he/s easy to
follow as he
sells heroin
in weighted
foil pouches

and when i scoop
him he yells "you
can/t hold me i/m
american" and when
i book him he asks
"how much is bail"
and pulls out his
plastic american
express card

Hans Jewinski

The Natural Thing

i go out at night
when the moon is new
hair grown long
and pockets full of poems

i carry strange birds on my shoulders
that sing and cry
thru the long night

walk with angels
when the wind is high
wings billowing around me
and long robes flowing

i am a stranger in the new fields
writing poems
from natural things

i gather
stars moon trees and rivers
shape them in my hands
as they urge me

'till they foam forth
a new
more natural thing

bp Nichol

Jacques Cartier

Cartier, Cartier
O Jacques Cartier
If you'd only steered clear
Of our wintery ways
Cartier, Cartier
O Jacques Cartier
If you'd just sailed that ship
On a summerside trip
Think what we'd have today!
  A Sherbrooke Street lined in coconut palms
  With flocks of parrots perched in their fronds
  Mount Royal covered in banana trees
  With cute little monkeys at play in their leaves
  And St. Lawrence swimming would be really grand
  Or just lying on the sand for a nice winter tan!

Cartier, Cartier
O Jacques Cartier
If you'd only steered clear
Of our wintery ways
Cartier, Cartier
O Jacques Cartier
If you'd just sailed that ship
On a summerside trip
Think what we'd have today!
  On Victoria Bridge, built of creepers and vines
  Shopping bags on our heads and laughing in time
  We'd make our barefoot way, O Jacques Cartier
  To the sound of tom-toms or the ukulele
  And orange orchids along Peel Street
  Mint, jasmine and lotus would smell so sweet!

Cartier, Cartier
O Jacques Cartier
If you'd only steered clear
Of our wintery ways
Cartier, Cartier
O Jacques Cartier
If you'd just sailed that ship
On a summerside trip
Think what we'd have today!
  Giraffes would stare on Pine Avenue
  At the squirrels there like things from a zoo
  White elephants stroll down De Lorimier like pets
  And Place Ville Marie with its slim minarets
  And blizzards of sand, hot, golden and clean
  Would make January drifts a great place to dream!

Cartier, Cartier
O Jacques Cartier
If you'd only steered clear
Of our wintery ways
Cartier, Cartier
O Jacques Cartier
If you'd just sailed that ship
On a summerside trip
Think what we'd have today!
  Montreal in Dakar, Tangiers or Conakry
  Montreal in Tokyo, Kyoto or Kobe
  Montreal in Aden, Freemantle or Bombay
  Montreal in Java, Borneo or Papeete
  Montreal in Phnom-Penh, in Bangkok or Hue
  Montreal in Hong Kong, Canberra or Sydney
Cartier, Cartier
O Jacques Cartier
Think what we'd have today!

Robert Charlebois, translated by Philip Stratford

Consomme and Coca Cola

Whenever I have a bowl of consomme which isn't any too often because I'm not particularly crazy about consomme I get to thinking about Gander. Gander is where I first tasted consomme. Funny about little things like that and how they bring certain other things to mind. Anyway this story isn't about consomme. At all. But it is about Gander. At least that's where it happened. In Gander.

Gander is a town in Newfoundland. But most people know it as an airport. As a matter of fact it used to be known as the crossroads of the world at one time. That was before the jets came along. You see before that all transatlantic flights had to stop over at Gander to refuel before going on to Shannon or New York or wherever. And in those days the airport terminal in Gander was a terrific place to go and watch all the people passing through. There used to be Indian princesses and nuns in garb you couldn't imagine the like of. And there was always someone very famous around too and if you were there you'd pretend you knew who they were even if you had never heard of them. Which was most likely. Some of the famous people who used to pass through Gander at the time were movie stars. And that's what this story is about really. Movie stars.

You see my father was a salesman and he used to work in Gander sometimes although we lived in Corner Brook. But he used to drive out there and stay a week or so at a time to sell cars for the Corner Brook Garage. And sometimes if it was during the summer when we didn't have to go to school he'd take us with him. My brothers and me.

That's how come Gord and Ken and I were there at this particular time. We were lounging around the terminal keeping an eye out for movie stars and things. You see I had once seen Alan Ladd there. Or at least I saw the back of his head. That had been on the last trip a couple of weeks before. And of course I had told Gord and Ken all about seeing Alan Ladd and about how he was so much shorter than in the movies. Though I'd never really been close enough to him to tell whether he was short or not. Actually I had read in a movie book about his being short and having to stand on boxes and things to do his love scenes. But anyway my telling about Alan Ladd had us all keen on seeing another movie star and we were giving every likely prospect a real going over, and saying things like what do you think and he looks like he might be and naw a movie star wouldn't dress like that and

anyways there'd be more people around him if he was and all sorts of stuff to help us decide. Well, while we were getting on with all this nonsense along comes this friend of my father's whose name was Sid which we always thought was kind of a stupid name for a girl to have. But anyway Sid comes along and asks us did we know William Lundigan was in the terminal. And we said no and who the hell is William Lundigan. So she explained that he was a movie star and that she had seen him in a picture called Inferno or something with Robert Ryan. And that he was down at the far end of the terminal with another movie star. But she didn't know her name.

Well we got pretty excited about that and pretty soon this bunch of people came walking by and Sid says to us there he is. It was no trouble to tell which one was William Lundigan because he was by far the most handsome of the lot. He really was. I mean he was tall and had light hair and he really was handsome. Even we could tell he was. And he was walking arm in arm with this blonde who must have been the most beautiful woman in the world. There were other people there too. Directors and things I guess they were.

While we were staring at them and Sid was saying things like isn't he a doll and things like that they walked right by us and went into the Big Dipper. The Big Dipper was the cocktail lounge of the terminal. We had been in there before with Dad and had coke while he was having a drink of rum or something. Actually I don't think children were allowed in there but Dad was a regular customer and when it wasn't too busy they didn't mind.

Anyway Sid left then and we just sat around wondering what it must be like to be a movie star and famous and everything. While we were wondering about it all one of the other men who had gone into the Big Dipper with William Lundigan came back out. He went over to the postcard counter and bought a couple of postcards to send back to his other movie star friends in Hollywood we figured. Well while he was writing on the postcards Gord got this brainwave that we should go over and talk to him. Which we did right off. Gord asked him excuse me sir but are you in there with William Lundigan and he said yes he was and how were we all in a Texas kinda voice. Then he left.

A minute or so later he was back telling us that Mr. Lundigan would like to see us and wouldn't we come on along with him. He led us into the Big Dipper and introduced us to all the people and

William Lundigan he asked us to sit down. He told us that the beautiful woman was Mari Aldon who had just finished making a movie with Gary Cooper called Drums of the Seminoles or something and that they were on their way to London to star in a picture together. And William Lundigan I guess was interested in fishing because he asked us all kinds of questions about the salmon rivers in Newfoundland and the best kinds of bait to use and all. And Gord and Ken answered most of the questions because I could hardly speak. Like my throat had gone dry and everything knowing that here I was sitting with these two movie stars.

So after talking about coming back to Newfoundland some day to do some salmon fishing Mr. Lundigan asked us if we would like a coke or something. Well our parents had always been pretty strict about good manners and we all said no thank you very much sir although I was dying to have a coke on account of my throat was so dry and everything. I guess he must have asked us a million times if we would let him buy us a coke or

something. But we knew our place and said no thank you very much sir every time. Which we figured was very polite.

An hour must have passed there with come on let me get you a coke and no thank you very much sir before my father came in. We introduced him to Mr. Lundigan and Miss Aldon and told him who they were before he said it was time for us to run along to the hotel which was just across the street from the terminal. We said good night and thank you to the movie stars and went out.

Back in the hotel room where we were staying we talked about what a nice bunch of people William Lundigan and Mari Aldon were and we would be sure to watch out for them in the movies from now on and then we went to bed.

I was feeling pretty terrific about it all except for one thing. I kept wishing that when I returned to Corner Brook I could think back that William Lundigan had bought me a coke. But he hadn't of course. Because I wouldn't let him. And even now all these years later it bugs me to think I wouldn't let William Lundigan do that for me. After all he was only trying to be nice.

Al Pittman

WILLY ASHWORTH

Hanging Loose in the Heavens

People call them suicidal crazies, say they have no decent respect for life. But hang gliders know better. They know that the will to fly is the opposite of a death wish.

Hang gliding is flight with no noise, no power, nothing but a kite, a mountain (the higher the better), and the wind. It is the purest form of flying available to man, the closest he has come to fulfilling the age-old wish for wings, perhaps the closest he can come to really feeling beauty and peace and independence. And it looks so natural, so easy.

Hang gliders say it *is* easy. Attached to each kite is a harness in which the pilot may sit or lie prone. To fly, all he need do is strap himself in, pick up his kite and either run into a prevailing wind for a natural lift-off, or leap from a cliff. Once in the air he soars with the wind, controlling direction, height and speed by moving his wings, just like a bird.

And once in the air man's power and independence is awesome. One man flew the trade winds in Hawaii for thirteen hours before falling darkness forced him down fifty-five miles from his starting point. And experienced fliers have found air lifts to carry them as high as 14,000 feet above ground.

Pilots insist that hang gliding, though an infant sport, is not a dangerous one. They say there is little danger at all unless a pilot ignores basic training or the rules of common sense and weather. It originated in California only ten years ago, an offshoot of a NASA engineer's attempts to design a re-entry device for space capsules, and very quickly acquired a world-wide following. In Canada today there are about 3,000 hang gliders and dozens of clubs, most of them near the mountains in the West. Pilots range in age from thirteen to seventy and spend an average of twenty-five to thirty-five hours a year in the air.

Last September a full team of Canadian pilots went to Kössen, Austria, for the first World Hang Gliding Championship, in which twenty-five countries participated. Our best performances came from Dean Kupchanko of Invermere, British Columbia, who placed second in his class, and Willi Mair of Montreal, who placed tenth in his class.

Those hang gliders who are competitive by nature will somehow get to South Africa for this year's world championship. And they will fly to win. But for most people, hang gliding remains a solo pleasure. For most people it is enough to liberate themselves from gravity, from the tensions and traffic jams of earthbound existence. It is enough to taste the heaven of absolute freedom, absolute control.

Joann Webb, *Weekend*

Dare-devil's-eye-view: Keith Abram, a member of
Tommy Bartlett's kite flying act, took this photo
while hanging 1,000 feet above the grandstand
at Stampede Park, Calgary.

Cool Wind from the North

You blew
Into my life
Like a cool wind
From the north
And you swept all
The deadwood
Away

You slipped
Into my dreams
Like a bird song
In the night
And you chased all
The shadows
Away

North wind, bird song
You took so long to fly
But now you're here
And I'm enchanted by
Your loving ways

You blew
Into my life
Like a cool wind
From the north
And you swept all
The deadwood away

North wind, bird song
You took so long to fly
But now you're here
And I'm enchanted by
Your loving ways

You slipped
Into my dreams
Like a bird song
In the night
And you chased all
The shadows
Away

Sylvia Fricker Tyson,
from her record *Cool Wind From the North*

The Stranger Song

It's true that all men you knew
Were dealers who said they were through
With dealing every time you gave them shelter.
I know that kind of man;
It's hard to hold the hand of anyone
Who's reaching for the sky just to surrender—
Who's reaching for the sky just to surrender.

And then sweeping up the jokers that
    he left behind,
You find he did not leave you very much—
Not even laughter.
Like any dealer, he was watching for the card
    that is so high and wild
He'll never need to deal another.
He was just some Joseph looking for a
    manger—
He was just some Joseph looking for a
    manger.

And then leaning on your window sill,
He'll say one day you caused his will
To weaken with your love and warmth
    and shelter
And then taking from his wallet
    an old schedule of trains, he'll say,
"I told you when I came I was a stranger—
I told you when I came I was a stranger."

But now another stranger
Seems to want to ignore his dreams
As though they were the burden of some other.
O you've seen that kind of man before,
His golden arm dispatching cards,
But now it's rusted from the elbow to
    the finger.
Yes, he wants to trade the game he knows
    for shelter.
You hate to watch another tired man
    lay down his hand, like he was
    giving up the holy game of poker,
And while he talks his dreams to sleep
You notice there's a highway that is
    curling up like smoke above his shoulder.
It's curling up like smoke above his shoulder.

You tell him to come in sit down
But something makes you turn around.
The door is open; you can't close your shelter;
You try the handle of the road.
It opens; do not be afraid.
It's you my love, you who are the stranger—
It is you my love, you who are the stranger.

Well, I've been waiting, I was sure
We'd meet between the trains we're waiting for.
I think it's time to board another.
Please understand, I never had a secret chart
To get me to the heart
Of this or any other matter.
When he talks like this
    you don't know what he's after.
When he speaks like this
    you don't know what he's after.

Let's meet tomorrow, if you choose,
Upon the shore, beneath the bridge
That they are building on some endless river.
Then he leaves the platform
For the sleeping car that's warm; you realize
He's only advertising one more shelter
And it comes to you, he never was a stranger
And you say, "OK, the bridge or someplace later."

Leonard Cohen

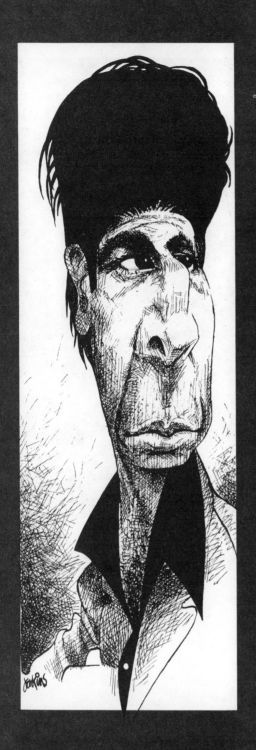

Hey, That's No Way
to Say Goodbye

I loved you in the morning
Our kisses deep and warm
Your hair upon the pillow
Like a sleepy golden storm
Yes many loved before us
I know that we are not new
In city and in forest
They smiled like me and you
But now it's come to distances
And both of us must try
Your eyes are soft with sorrow
Hey, that's no way to say goodbye.

I'm not looking for another
As I wander in my time
Walk me to the corner
Our steps will always rhyme,
You know my love goes with you
As your love stays with me,
It's just the way it changes
Like the shoreline and the sea,
But let's not talk of love or chains
And things we can't untie,
Your eyes are soft with sorrow
Hey, that's no way to say goodbye.

I loved you in the morning
Our kisses deep and warm
Your hair upon the pillow
Like a sleepy golden storm
Yes, many loved before us
I know that we are not new
In city and in forest
They smiled like me and you
But let's not talk of love or chains
And things we can't untie,
Your eyes are soft with sorrow
Hey, that's no way to say goodbye.

Leonard Cohen

Downtown Streets

There are still people
who write each other
intimate letters who
sing their personal arias
to an audience of white
paper; is it pain they
score, bursts of light they
note after a dark illness,
a childish jump, or some
mongrel dance-step in the
icicled rooms of snow?

Sometimes I still stand
outside a lighted window
on downtown streets (just
as I used to thirty years
ago) a woman sits at a
table writing intimate
letters, she is asking, *do
you really like the smell
of my perfume*, she is saying
*next time you come it will
be winter the season of
mandarin oranges.*

Standing there under
the window
I think I can hear
the sound
of her ghostly pen
moving across the page.
I think I can hear it
singing
in the downtown streets.

Miriam Waddington

Quiet

Quiet as the world after midnight
quiet, quiet is my thought of you.

I wait till all the people are asleep
so my thought can touch you, you, only you.

let this be my poem to you
you, you you, only you.

Miriam Waddington

Ending

The big winds
of the world
have been called up
from sleep   they are
cross   shake thunder
and rain over the
city   spit out
teeth of ice from
their angry mouths.

I stand alone
in the great anteroom
no use now
even to be afraid
there is no one to
be afraid to anymore.

Miriam Waddington

When I was a Little Girl

When I was a little girl
We used to walk together
Tim, my brother who wore glasses,
And I, holding hands
Tightly as we crossed the bridge
And he'd murmur, "You pray now"
—being a clergyman's son—
Until the big white boys
Had kicked on past.
Later we'd climb the bluffs
Overhanging the ghost town
And pick the small white lilies
And fling them like bombers
Over Slocan

Joy Kogawa

Maiden Aunt

1

Seems all right if the going down
to die happens at home
where blood and relatives
can dandle the emptying body
safe from the alien click and
snapping shut of clinics.

The trappings
of an event bring in the family.
I am an event in passing, lying here
not wearing the proper colour for the time of day,
not stressed and strutted for the occasion.
Everything I was set out to do
is done; every possession accorded
my right to stay within the family.
It's knowing one's place that's important,
from six feet down to three storeys up,
the length and width of the boundaries.
This business of dying
is only a process, a sort
of making room.
It's all right knowing
where and with whom I'll lie
I have my place, relinquish nothing
but then I've reconnoitered for years.

11

She is too newly lain here
by the rowan to need another
mark. Not that there was anything
particular to remember, just gentle
slightly remote maidenliness
of late grown slightly faint.
Unlike her to strike into
our lives with a single
unthought act, she who was just there
still there under the rowan
and then we've raised a mark
it will be the only one
to her, unfamiliar.

Anne Corkett

Forerunners

In the summer of 1947 I stayed at Victoria Beach where I was collecting folklore for the National Museum of Canada. I was told that I should see Mr. A.B. Thorne for an experience that no other member of his family would talk about. My companion was the author and poet, Martha Banning Thomas. The evening of our call was fine and pleasant, with a warm summer breeze drifting in our car windows. We drove the narrow, hilly road in the spirit of sweet companionship, little realizing that our return trip would be far from serene, or that our thoughts for many a night afterwards would be in a turmoil.

The Thorne house is at Karsdale, a white frame cottage with a garden that is always filled in summer with beautiful flowers. Mrs. Thorne is the gardener, and she knows the botanical name of everything she grows. The interior of the house shows the care of loving hands with its hooked and braided mats, antimacassars, cloths with crocheted edges, and embroidered cushion covers. She also has treasures of old china handed down in her family and cherished through the years. It is a dainty, pleasant house, and she and her husband are a gracious host and hostess, making their visitors feel at home immediately.

Mr. Thorne is a man of medium height with blue eyes, an aquiline nose, and a rather sensitive mouth. Now probably in his sixties, he can still dig garden or ditch in a way that would shame many a younger man. Yet with work to occupy him, and an excellent wife to care for all his needs, he appears to be a singularly nervous man. This is little wonder, considering the experience of his youth which we had come to hear.

We had a short period of conversation until the proper atmosphere was established, and then we asked Mr. Thorne if he would tell his story. After a little hesitation he began.

"I hope I'll never have to go through that racket again," he said. "Well I'll tell you. I had just come home from the States and I had a friend whose name was Joe Holmes. We were always together when I was home, but Joe wasn't very strong. We were young men then, about twenty, and one evening we were together and I had a letter to mail. We hadn't been drinking. I don't want you to think we had because we hadn't, and we didn't imagine what we saw. About ten o'clock we took the letter to the post office. It was in the Riordens' house, the way people often have them in the country. I lived at Thorne's Cove this side of it, and Joe lived two houses away on the other side.

"Well, we mailed the letter, and then we sat alongside the road opposite the house and talked. It was a bright night with a full moon, and it was too nice to separate and go home so early. The Riordens' grass was about three feet high at that time, and there was a turnip field behind it. We heard a hoe strike against a rock and it attracted our attention. We sat forward then and looked and, to our surprise, we saw a Thing come crawling on its hands and feet from the southeast corner of the house. Then it stood up and we could see that it was a man. We were on the lower or south side of the road, and it was on the upper or north side. Then it went out of sight.

"In the country we often think a lot without saying anything, and anyway there's often no need of words between friends. So we just sat there and didn't say anything, and before long it came out again. We didn't move an inch, but we watched, and this time it came halfway across the road. The time for keeping quiet was over now, so I said, 'Joe, did you see that?' He said yes, he did, and by this time it had gone back again. You might think we'd had enough, but we kept still and it didn't keep us waiting very long.

"The third time was like the others. It came out and went back. We still sat there and in a second's time it was back and it went under the cherry tree. There were more apple trees on our side of the road then than now, and they took to shaking and the apples fell to the ground. I was frightened by this time and I said, 'Joe, I've got to go home.' That would have been all right if we'd both lived in the same direction. Probably we'd have left even before that, but we were braver together. We decided to go to Joe's house and we started to run. Joe wasn't very strong as I said, but he always thought he could run, and he could, and I was afraid I couldn't keep up with him. I guess the fear got into my feet because I ran just as fast as he did.

"When we got to his house we stood in the road and talked. We were young men and curious, and we didn't like to leave it there because it would always pester us and we'd never know what we'd seen. It didn't seem like a prank, but if it was, we wanted to settle it. Finally I said, 'Let's go back; I'm not afraid.' I wasn't either, so long as Joe was with me. Nothing was going to hurt the two of us and besides, it's easy to be brave when you have company. 'We'll see what it is,' I said. So we walked back and pretty soon we saw it and it was coming to meet us. It was halfway between the Riordens and the Cronins, and that's the next house, the one in between. I said, 'There it is; don't leave me.' As I said, I figured that with two of us it couldn't do much harm and I wanted to find out what it was. I meant to touch it and then I'd know for sure if it was real. When we were within twenty feet of it I said again, 'Joe, don't leave me,' and then I walked up till my face was close beside it. I'll never forget that moment as long as I live.

"It had on black pants, a white shirt with a hard bosom front, and black braces. Its head was bare and he was of medium size. It looked as though its eyes were deeply sunk in, and they were very bright and penetrating, and the only thing it looked like was a skeleton. I didn't touch it, although I would have even then, but Joe gave a scream and ran, and I was scared. I wasn't long overtaking him, and from that time Joe had a hard time to keep up with me. It followed and kept twenty feet behind us. There were bars on the Holmes fence. We jumped them, and the Thing cut across the field to head us off, but we got there first. We stood in the doorway and watched it for half an hour. There was a stone wall with a rotten pole on top of it, and it stood on this pole. In the morning I went out and felt that pole and, do you know, it was so rotten it just crumbled up in my hands. Why that pole was so rotten it couldn't have held a bird.

"As I said, I'll never forget that racket as long as I live, and as for Joe, he would never talk of it except to his mother and to me. A year later he was taken sick and a while later he died, and he always claimed this was a forerunner for him. We were both sure it couldn't have been anybody playing tricks because the moon was full and we could see everything as plain as in the day.

"Then a strange thing happened. Joe died of a tubercular throat, and he died hard, but he never rambled in his mind. It was always clear right to the end. But one day not long before his death Joe said to his mother, 'My throat won't hurt me any more. He (the apparition) was here and rubbed it.' The pain had been almost more than he could bear, but from that moment it stopped and he never felt it in his throat again. I sat up with him every night, and do you know what he looked like when he died? He looked just like that man, for he was pretty well wasted away."

Was this then the explanation, and had Joe seen his own apparition as he was to appear in death? Was that the meaning of it all?

When Mr. Thorne was through we sat quietly and, after a while, I said jokingly that he would be telling me soon what colour the man's eyes were. To my surprise he took this seriously and pondered the matter. Finally he said, "No I can't quite do that," but his hesitation showed how vivid the experience was even to that day which would be forty or more years after the event.

When the story was over Mrs. Thorne gave us a hot drink and some cookies and we started back to Victoria Beach. The country road was very dark

that night and there was no moon to comfort
us—nor to show us this unwelcome figure either.
As we came to the Riorden house Miss Thomas
said, "Now that is where they sat," pointing to the
bank on the south side of the road, "and that is
where they saw it," pointing north.

"Yes, Martha," I said, pressing the accelerator a
little harder.

"And this," as we approached the Cronin house,
"is where it stood in the road and they saw it
clearly."

"Yes, Martha," driving faster still.

"And that is where it must have stood on the
wall," she said as we reached the Holmes property.
I relaxed a little then glad enough to be away from
that district, for I wanted no more of the
supernatural that night.

A year later I attended a service in the Karsdale
church and the Thornes stood almost opposite me
as we sang that lovely hymn, "Unto the Hills."
When we came to the line, "No moon shall harm
thee in the silent night," I looked at Mr. Thorne
who has been a nervous man since this incident and
thought, "But the moon did harm him." Or at least
it revealed what the ghost was like, and the effect
has never worn off. Would his nervousness be due
only to the fright of a moonlit night in his youth, or
does he fear that when his time comes the
apparition will appear as his forerunner too? It is a
question I have never liked to ask him.

Helen Creighton,
from *Bluenose Ghosts*

Shanadithit

What I know of you
is only what my grade seven history book
told me
that you were young when they caught you
that your people lived in deerhide houses
that you drew lovely pictures
that they changed your name to Nancy
that you died soon after
that you were the last of the Beothuks

you probably didn't know that
did you
that you were the last of your people
that when you went
there was no one to take your place
I suppose you died
thinking there were uncles and cousins
with toothaches and babies
that there were hunters
young men you'd like to be with
coming home game-laden to campfires
on the shore of the lake
your executioners called Red Indian

you didn't know you'd end up
in my grade seven history book
did you

and when you died your lonely death
when the white disease put an end to you
you didn't know
that one of the generation of poets
would have given his soul
to be with you
to tell you he wouldn't forget
you didn't know that I would have kissed you
and cried when you went
of course that has all to do
with my own images of you
and they are much too mixed up
with technicolor movies
and my own boyish musings

I see you as beautiful as Debra Paget
who played the role of an Indian girl
in a movie I barely remember
I can't see you
no matter how hard I try
mud-caked and offensive smelling
I can't see you groaning and twisting
on the floor of your smoky wigwam
locked in any embrace
with your rough raw-boned cousins.

I see you
(and I know this is all wrong)
leaning over a blue pool
and sun filters through the alders
and sends little shivers of light
bouncing off your golden thigh
where your beautifully embroidered dress
(like the one marked yours in the St. John's museum)
parts to let you bend
your reflection looks up at me
from the still water
and your eyes are two hollows
deeper than any this brook could fill
the eyes of a martyr
of one who waits patiently for death
knowing that the history books
and the poor poets must finally have their day

yet in all this
there is a sadness about you
for you had not always consented to your martyrdom
before this
before it had all been revealed to you
through witchcraft and religion
you had wished rather
that I would walk buckskinned into your forest
and take you with me
upstream to a place
the shaman and the gods had ordained for us
and there in an eternity of summers
we would have loved each other gently
in the brook-cooled summer sun

that dream of course
(though it pleases me that you had it)
was entirely impossible
for you had to die as you did
you had to be the last of your race
before I could love you at all

I admit now (putting this poem aside)
that my weakness has nothing whatever
to do with you
(not as you were or might have been
in those few of your own dead end days)
it's the girl born glowing
out of the wild wood of my boyhood
who's kept me warmly captive
all these slow growing years
she rather than you
keeps me spinning out of time
keeps me soaring in the centuries
keeps me searching like a child
for separate lives
as real (at least) as this
with an extra touch of magic.

Al Pittman

Two men came to a hole in the sky. One asked the other to lift him up. If only he would do so, then he in turn would lend him a hand.

His comrade lifted him up, but hardly was he up when he shouted aloud for joy, forgot his comrade and ran into heaven.

The other could just manage to peep in over the edge of the hole; it was full of feathers inside. But so beautiful was it in heaven that the man who looked in over the edge forgot everything, forgot his comrade whom he had promised to help and simply ran off into all the splendour of heaven.

Inugpasugjuk, Eskimo shaman

Lines for Ohiyesa, the Sioux

*"All who have lived
much out of doors, know
that there is a magnetic
and nervous force that
accumulates in solitude"*

You are alone
in forests
the snow is quiet
there are trees
there is nothing
like emptiness
anywhere
you walk
with no words
even shadows
are more than darkness
skin floats
on the bones of stars
your dream
returns
over and over

Gail Fox

The Witch Canoe

"You won't believe what I'm going to tell you, but I give you my word as a cook (don't laugh over there in the corner, you young rascals, you) that every word I am telling you is the truth, and that it happened to me about fifty years ago. Maybe I've not had much of an education, but you over there, don't forget you're nothing but ignorant scum. Sure. Sure. You'll find out that there always have been, and always will be, strange things in this world that can't be explained: to float in the air, for example, like a little log on the Gatineau River."

In order to judge the effect of these words, the old cook glanced around the semicircle of rough-looking men gathered about his enormous stove which gave off such a pleasant warmth and such good smells. With the gesture of an officiating priest he lifted the cover from a large cauldron in which pork and beans were simmering and seemed satisfied with the perfume which enveloped his nose. Moving to another pot he stirred vigorously at a bubbling mixture, then drew forth, like a magician, a fine light "pull" of maple candy to celebrate, at midnight, the arrival of the New Year. In the lumber camps on the Gatineau he was called, with a cruel good nature, Joe la Bosse, for he had become quite humpbacked with age. Outside, the snow came halfway up the building, a sub-zero cold had set the trees crackling, and from time to time the thin, sharp cries of hungry wolves tore the air with piercing notes. All this gave a homely worth to the hard beds covered with woolen blankets, the rude tables of a restful brown, chairs worn and polished like bone, and to the tantalizing smells and pleasant warmth of the camp. The little barrel of rum, a gift from the foreman to help celebrate this lonely New Year's Day, was set on the table as if it were enthroned, and seemed somehow to mock the homesickness of the lonely lumbermen. Certainly they could not forget their wives, their families and the music and gaiety they were missing, but they would find them all in the spring and in the meantime they would make the best of it and put a bold face on their misfortune. The rum, the warmth of the camp, the beans and the candy and the stories of Joe la Bosse all helped.

Now he was getting ready to tell one of those stores of his and everyone was glad, for Joe la Bosse knew well how to hold his audience, with his lively glance, his spirited gestures and his miraculous tales. He settled himself at the foot of a long table in his favourite nook, pulled off his boots and stretched out his feet in their thick woolen socks to the end of the bench and snapped his braces over an enormous red-checked shirt. Then, sensing that he had his audience well in hand, he began by asking a question.

"Have you ever heard tell of witch canoes?"

"Yes," answered one young logger with a wide-awake look. "Those are canoes that travel in the air and are driven by the devil. They had them long ago. They carried those who were possessed by demons, especially loggers."

The lumbermen began to laugh noisily. Joe la Bosse interrupted sharply. "Don't laugh my friends. Perhaps one day people will ride through the air as we today ride in buggies and sleds along the King's Highway. But fifty or a hundred years ago, or even in olden times, you could travel in the air only on a magic carpet or astride a witch's broom or in a canoe, a witch canoe—all diabolical methods."

He took a long rest then began his story.

I had just turned nineteen. It was my fourth winter in the lumber camp. I was not a blasphemer, but I had a weakness for women that almost brought about my damnation. It was New Year's Eve and it wasn't little goblets that they passed the rum in that night, but little tubs. Full as an egg I was, stretched out on my bed with all my clothes on. Suddenly, I came to with a start. Someone was leaning over me. I looked into the big face of Jack Boyd, the foreman. No one had seen him before that year, but it was he who had bought rum for all of us for New Year's Day and he had the air of a man with money.

"Wouldn't you like to see your girl?" he asked me. I looked at him stupidly, full of drink and sleep.

"Wake up, then," he told me, shaking me with all his might, for he was as strong as two horses. "Do you want to see your Lise tonight?"

See my Lise. That was impossible. She lived at Lavaltrie, my own village, more than a hundred leagues away. I was bored to death. I would have made the journey on foot and in the depth of winter just to see her, but I could not leave the camp. Worse than that, I would have sold my soul to the devil just to spend one night with her. And that was what almost happened that night.

"Don't make me laugh," I said to Boyd. "Lavaltrie is more than a hundred leagues away. It would take days to make the journey on foot, or even in a horse and sleigh."

"Oh there's no question of that," said Jack Boyd. "We'll make the journey by air, in a canoe. In two hours we'll be at Lavaltrie. We can go to a dance in the village, there's sure to be one somewhere tonight, and at six o'clock tomorrow morning we'll be back in camp."

A chill ran down my spine. "What! Are we going to take the witch canoe?"

"Call it what you like m'lad," Boyd said with a smile. "That's of no importance. The main thing is to have a good time tonight. Now, to take the witch canoe there must be an even number—two, four, six or eight. There are seven ready to go tonight, you will be the eighth. Hurry up, the men are waiting outside for us and there's not a minute to lose." Then, as if he had known in advance what I would say, he added, "But before we leave, so as not to arouse any suspicions, you must behave just as usual. On the stroke of midnight you must jump the New Year in, over the barrel of lard, for you are the youngest in the camp."

I, however, was too dazed by the rum.

"Too drunk you mean," shouted a young fellow in the midst of laughter already thickened by drink.

"Drunk or not it's none of your business, but if you want me to go on with the story you must treat me with more respect, my young puppy."

"Look, grandpère, we really want to hear your story. Please go on. Ti-Paul will apologize."

Ti-Paul begged pardon with good grace and the cook continued.

All right then. At any rate, I couldn't jump the barrel as I had in other years. The men ended by accepting my excuses. Jack Boyd and I and two others went out. The sky was clear, the stars shone to lift our spirits. But the cold was such that it made the trees moan. A slim, dark canoe lay on the snow near a cord of wood. Four men from a neighbouring camp were waiting for us, their paddles in their hands.

"Baptiste, you know the canoe. You steer." ordered Jack Boyd.

Baptiste settled himself in the stern of the canoe. Before I had time to think about it, I found myself with the others in the little boat, my paddle in my hand.

Baptiste addressed us in a loud voice. "We are all going to take an oath to the devil, and this, you understand, is no joke. It is very solemn. But I know from experience that if you do what I tell you, we'll pull through. Pay good heed to what I'm going to say. To begin with, there must be no swearing and no drinking. Then, it is forbidden to

speak the name of God or to touch the cross on a steeple—even to brush against it with the canoe or with the paddles during the voyage. Is that understood?"

"Yes, yes," repeated the men in chorus.

"All right then," went on Baptiste. "Repeat with me: Satan, ruler of Hell, we promise to surrender our souls to you, if, within the next six hours, we pronounce the name of God, your Lord and ours, or if we touch a cross on our journey. On this condition, you will transport us through the air, wherever we want to go, and you will bring us back again to camp. *Acabris! Acabras! Acabram!* Make us travel over the mountains."

We had hardly said the words with Baptiste when we felt the canoe rise into the air above the camp, over the trees, and before long, over the mountains. Each paddle stroke sent the canoe shooting like an arrow through the wind. The air beat in our faces, engraving them with moustaches and masks like raccoons', and giving our noses the appearance of badly cooked black sausage. The forest now looked to us like enormous patches of terrifying shadows on blindingly white snow. Before long we saw a great serpent, shining like a mirror, which threw us the reflections of the moonbeams. This was the Gatineau. Then dwellings appeared, all very tiny from where we were and blending so well with the snow around them that we could only distinguish them by the faint glow coming from the windows. Then we began to see little villages and church steeples which stood straight up, piercing the sky like lances. For a long time we flew above forests and villages, rivers and lakes, so fast that we left them behind us like a trail of smoke. Then we saw thousands of little lights, all close together as if to keep each other warm. This was Montreal. It all gave me a very strange feeling.

Baptiste knew the route well. He guided us straight to Lavaltrie. All at once he called to us, "Pay attention, all of you. We're going to come down in the field of my godfather, Jean-Jean Gabriel. There we are sure to find out what parties or dances are going on in the neighborhood. *Bramaca! Irbaca!*"

At once, after these magic words, the canoe dived to the ground and landed heavily on a snowbank near the woodlot of Jean-Jean Gabriel. We left in Indian file for the village for we had to make a path through the thick snow. We knocked at the door of Baptiste's godfather, but all the family had left for some celebration or other. The hired girl who answered the door told us that the old people were having a snack with the Robillards and that the younger ones were at Batissette Auge's at Petite Misère at the bottom of Contrecoeur on the other side of the river, where they were having a New Year's party.

"Let us go to Batissette's," we shouted in chorus. We went back to the canoe.

"Acabris! Acabras! Acabram! Let us ride over the mountains," cried Baptiste once more. And off we set, flung aloft like the renegades we were. Two strokes of the paddle and presto! we were on the other side of the river, above the brightly lighted house of Batissette Auge. Muffled sounds of a fiddle and bursts of laughter rose to meet us and we could see dancing shadows on the thickly frosted windows. All this spurred us on.

We hid the canoe not far from the house and hurried towards the warmth, the dancing, the songs and the laughter, the girls and the merry-making. Baptiste warned us not to drink and to guard our tongues well.

"Above all," he told us, "not a glass of beer or of spirits. And remember, when I give the sign follow me at once. Don't forget that in six hours we must be back at camp or it will be the worse for us. You hear me, my lads?"

Poor old Baptiste, he led the way. He was the courageous one. The rest of us held back. Then, all at once, we felt reassured and knocked impatiently on the Auge's door. It was Batisette's father who opened the door to us and welcomed us with open arms. We knew almost everyone there. They threw questions at us, for the whole village was amazed to see us there, when they had imagined us to be more than a hundred leagues away.

Baptiste did his best to deal with the questions—at least for the first fifteen minutes, for after that he was so well soaked that there was no use asking him anything. As for me, I had caught sight of my Lise who was dancing with a young boyfriend from Lanoraie, by the name of Boisjoli. I went up to her and asked if I could have the next dance. I had become very shy in front of her, so that I appeared awkward and rude. But, as I told you at the start, I didn't swear; I just blushed right up to my ears. Pretending not to notice this (the sly girl was a lot sharper than I was even then) she accepted with a smile, which made me forget that I had risked my soul's safety for the pleasure of dancing with her for a few short hours.

For two glorious hours we danced together, one dance right after another without stopping. I was tireless and so was she. Jack Boyd offered me a glass of whisky. I turned it down. How could he

offer us drinks when he knew we had been warned not to touch them? I couldn't understand it and wondered more and more as I saw him passing from one to another with his bottle, offering a glass here and a glass there. He even offered one to Baptiste, who was long since full as a goat.

At a given moment, Boyd came to warn me that we must be on our way and that there must be no stopping to say goodbye, for fear of attracting attention. I didn't want to go. I wanted to stay with my Lise.

"Nothing doing," he told me. "Eight we came, eight we return—the whole damned gang together."

So we left like savages, one after another, so as to escape notice.

"Acabris! Acabras! Acabram! Make us rise over the mountains."

Our canoe rose without difficulty. We followed the same route for our return to camp, along the Gatineau, but this time with all sorts of zigzags and monkey business, for our poor Baptiste was feeling so sure of himself now. He was drunk as a pig and we had to keep rousing him (there was nothing else to do for he was the only one who knew the way) and when we would get him awake he cursed like a lost soul, but happily for us he never pronounced the name of God. If he had, we would have taken a pretty plunge—no doubt right down to the fires of hell. I tremble even now when I think of it. We skirted churches, belfries, crosses—yes, even a temperance cross which a bishop had caused to be set up but without actually touching any of them. There must have been a good angel watching over us.

At last we saw the long white serpent of the Gatineau, but it was not gleaming as it had been when we started, for the moon was hidden behind heavy dark clouds. We could just make out the river by the rows of dark pines on the two banks.

What a hurry I was in to get there! I was filled with dark foreboding and my spirits sank like a

gherkin in vinegar. What had possessed me to risk
my immortal soul for a few hours of dancing with
my Lise? And especially when, one year later, she
was to marry that young Boisjoli of Lanoraie, the
fellow who was with her at the party when I came
up and asked her to dance? Probably she was glad
to be rid of a boor, who didn't even have the
manners to come and say goodbye to her. And
what still bothers me is that I shall never know. I
was angry with Jack Boyd, Baptiste and most of
all myself, the stupid blockhead.

As we approached the camp, Baptiste made a bad manoeuvre. The canoe took a dive and caught on a large spruce tree, spilling us all out. There we were dropping from branch to branch, until we tumbled head first into a bank of snow. My friend Baptiste swore like a demon, but it didn't matter now. We were safe. My first thought was to thank heaven, but I ask myself now: was it really the good Lord who protected us, or the devil who didn't want us?

But the most curious part of the story is that the next day there was no Jack Boyd. He had disappeared. No one ever saw him again. And that morning, when I recalled the night's adventure to Baptiste and the others, not one of them remembered a thing about it. The rascals, they had drunk too much.

The youngest member of the audience was asleep with his head on the table, but the others raised their glasses of rum to the health of Joe la Bosse, the best storyteller in the lumber camps.

Midnight had struck and in the low, dark room the beans gave out an odour that was, alas, only too familiar but still tantalizing and Joe la Bosse, magician that he was, drew forth from the big cauldron of brown and bubbling maple syrup, long, blond, shining ribbons of candy which he cut into sweet and delicious little bonbons.

From *The Magic Fiddler*, by Claude Aubry

A Message from the Management:

Macleod Hotel Rules and Regulations (Adopted unanimously by the Proprietor, September 1, 1882 A.D.)

- Guests will be provided with breakfast and dinner, but must rustle their own lunch.
- Spiked boots and spurs must be removed at night before retiring.
- Dogs are not allowed in the Bunks, but may sleep underneath.
- Candles, hot water and other luxuries charged extra, also towels and soap.
- Towels changed weekly. Insect Powder for sale at the bar.
- Crap, Chuck Luck, Stud Horse Poker and Black Jack games are run by the management. Indians and niggers charged double rates.
- Special Rates to "Gospel Grinders" and the "Gambling Perfesh."
- Every known fluid (water excepted) for sale at the bar.
- A deposit must be made before towels, soap or candles can be carried to rooms. When boarders are leaving, a rebate will be made on all candles or parts of candles not burned or eaten.
- Two or more persons must sleep in one bed when so requested by the proprietor.
- Not more than one dog allowed to be kept in each single room.
- Baths furnished free down at the river, but bathers must furnish their own soap and towels.
- No kicking regarding the quality or quantity of meals will be allowed; those who do not like the provender will get out, or be put out.
- Assaults on the cook are strictly prohibited.
- Quarrelsome or boisterous persons, also those who shoot off without provocation guns or other explosive weapons on the premises, and all boarders who get killed, will not be allowed to remain in the House.
- When guests find themselves or their baggage thrown over the fence, they

may consider that they have received notice to quit.

- Jewelry and other valuables will not be locked in the safe. This hotel has no such ornament as a safe.
- The proprietor will not be accountable for anything.
- In case of FIRE the guests are requested to escape without unnecessary delay.
- The BAR in the Annex will be open day and night. All Day drinks, 50 cents each; Night drinks, $1.00 each. No Mixed Drinks will be served except in case of death in the family.
- Only regularly registered guests will be allowed the special privilege of sleeping on the Bar Room floor.
- Guests without baggage must sleep in the vacant lot, and board elsewhere until their baggage arrives.
- Guests are forbidden to strike matches or spit on the ceiling, or to sleep in bed with their boots on.
- No cheques cashed for anybody. Payment must be made in Cash, Gold Dust, or Blue Chips.
- Saddle horses can be hired at any hour of the Day or Night, or the next day or night if necessary.
- Meals served in own rooms will not be guaranteed in any way. Our waiters are hungry and not above temptation.
- To attract attention of waiters or bell boys, shoot a hole through the door panel. Two shots for ice water, three for a deck of cards, and so on.
- All guests are requested to rise at 6 a.m. This is imperative as the sheets are needed for tablecloths.
- No tips must be given to any waiters or servants. Leave them all with the proprietor, and he will distribute them if it is considered necessary.
- Everything Cash in Advance. Following Tariff subject to change:
- Board—$25.00 per month.
- Board and Lodging—$50.00 per month, with wooden bench to sleep on.
- Board and Lodging—$60.00 per month, with bed to sleep on.

Quoted in *Colombo's Little Book of Canadian Proverbs, Graffiti, Limericks, and other Vital Matters*, by J. R. Colombo.

Plastic Grass, Aluminum Seats . . . Debased Ball?

Until the other night, I hadn't been to a ballgame since Nat King Cole sat a few rows in front of me. That makes it about a dozen years between games.

The first ball game I went to, in the old Maple Leaf Stadium, would have been another dozen years before that. That day Sam Jethro stole a base, which made him my favourite, a position he maintained throughout the waning years of his career.

In those days my bedtimes were more rigorously observed than now, but I managed to negotiate an arrangement whereby I stayed up to hear Jethro's first at-bat on the old fictionalized CKEY game broadcasts. These consisted of the announcer reading the play-by-play code off the news wire and embellishing it as he saw fit. In the background was a tape loop of crowd hubbub interspersed with cheers. They even had the sound of the bat hitting the ball. Or maybe I provided that.

Jethro and I grew older that way, me staying up ever later while he slipped farther down the batting order. At the Sunday double-headers I watched as he was shifted from centre-field to left field, then to right field, to "utility" outfielder, to pinch runner. My father, who took me to the games, brought along the week's newspapers. He would look up if there were two out, or if the count was full, or if the bases were loaded.

Baseball was one thing to me and quite another to my father. For him it recalled old wars with his father, grandpa's old world versus my father's new. Grandfather Bossin was scornful of such frivolities as baseball. A boy old enough to play ball was old enough to have a job. "But pa," my father argued, "Babe Ruth earns $50,000 a year." Grandfather Bossin was incredulous. "For doing that?" he said.

In those days Toronto was organized into baseball teams differentiated primarily by race. My father's brother told me that when the Jews played in Christie Pits they carried extra bats for the walk from the diamond to the streetcar.

The Leafs meanwhile were playing at Hanlan's Point and, to beat the crowds, men would leap to shore from the ferry before the gang-plank was down.

By my day things were calmer, though crowded still. My father, if he wasn't reading the papers, would meet up with a bunch of his cronies and sit talking politics in the cool breeze off the lake. I rooted for Sam Jethro.

But soon Jethro retired and it wasn't long before his team-mates followed: Stan Jock, Lou Morton, Hector Rodriguez, Archie Wilson, Mike Goliat, Rocky Nelson. With them went the crowds, including my father's. Then mine. The team was sold and shortly after it folded. My father died. The stadium was torn down.

There had been something genteel and even contemplative about those baseball games, something that was lost for a time.

So it wasn't a victory I was looking for the other night when I went down to see the Blue Jays. It wasn't a victory I found either, nor was it anything that much resembled baseball as the Leafs played it on Fleet Street.

The colour of the grass was off. The field, astro-turf on concrete, was too flat. The earth for the base paths and the pitcher's mound was imported. Halfway through the game attendants came onto the field to sweep the dirt back off the grass.

With the exception of the baseball bats there wasn't a stick of wood in the stadium. The benches were aluminum, the fences plastic.

The old hoardings are of course gone. No Blue Jay batter will receive a wrist-watch for hitting the People's Credit Jewellers sign, nor can he win one hundred dollars by popping the ball through the O in "Stoney's Used Cars on the Danforth".

Now the billboards hawk nationally distributed products to the TV audience. And the lights, set up for television, are arranged so that no-one casts a shadow.

Though I wasn't far from the players, they seemed a long way off, a feeling that brought to mind an Inuit woman who once approached me after a concert in Aklavik. She asked if I would let her daughter touch me to prove to the little girl that I was not on TV.

Sitting in the stands, in the cool breezes of the lakeshore, in the Toronto twilight, I knew that what had meant one thing to my father, then another to me, now had become something entirely different again.

Nonetheless I have a new favourite. He is Steven Staggs, the Blue Jays' second baseman. He came to bat with two out, two men on base and Toronto two runs behind. This is what he did.

Staggs took the first pitch for strike one. He then let the second pitch go by, which was also a strike. This led someone in the stands to offer a suggestion that had not changed since Sam Jethro's days. Still Staggs stood his ground watching two more pitches go by, both outside the strike zone. Someone near me wondered out loud if

the man had died. But young Staggs is evidently not one led easily into temptaion. The fifth pitch was not to his liking either, nor the umpire's, and there was Staggs facing a full count with two men out and two men on. The atmosphere changed as 18,000 fans realized that this encounter signified more than they had thought. The criticism ceased. My father's spirit had stirred from its papers. The pitcher threw the ball and Staggs handled it masterfully. He never budged. The umpire called, "Ball four", and Staggs walked to first base.

I don't know that I'll go to any more games, but I will keep an ear cocked for young Staggs' progress. I like his style.

Bob Bossin

The Olympic Dream Game

I hear there's money to be made
Gonna write an Olympic song for the parade
Twenty grand would feel good in my hand
Here's hopin' old Drapeau will understand

I got me a ticket in the lottery
You know I'm a winner, gonna take the wife to dinner
Gonna help the girls and boys make a little noise
Down in Montreal
In the stadium
Down in Montreal

I'm gonna buy myself some beautiful money
You know I want to join, buy Olympic coins
Got the flag on my car, high protein candy bar
Going down to Montreal
In the summertime
Going down to Montreal

Come to the Games
People gettin' ready all around the world
Fortune and fame
People roasting weinies on the Olympic flame

I was never one for playin' at sports
Maybe it's because I had the wrong kind of shorts
But here's my chance to get some joggin' pants
And join the crowd down in Mont-royal
With the family
Down in Mont-royal

Peut-être nous chanterons en français?
Maybe in Ukaranian? Let's sing it in Canadian.

No matter what we say
You know I want to be there for the judgment day

Come to the Games
People gettin' ready all around the world
Sun or the rain
We never mind the weather when it's good times together

Come to the Games
Sun or the rain
It's never win or lose, it's how you play the game
Come to the Games.

The Pied Pumkin

Mail Sortin' Man

And he went
Montreal Orillia Wawa Mississauga
Coburg Moose Jaw Killaloe Fort Frances
Salmon Arm and Lake Louise
Winnipeg Prince Albert Truro
Tuktoyaktuk Renfrew Flin Flon
Katchican Inuvik Kamloops Churchill Bramalea

Well the memo said to John Henry
Gonna bring me a steam sorter down
Gonna put that steam sorter out on the job
Gonna wop that mail on down Lord, Lord
Wop that mail on down.

John Henry said to the memo
A man ain't nothing but a man
And before I let that old sorter beat me down
I'll die with a letter in my hand Lord, Lord,
Die with a letter in my hand.

Now the man who made the steam sorter
Thought he was mighty fine
But John Henry sorted out fifteen bags
And the steam sorter only done nine Lord, Lord,
Steam sorter only done nine.

And it went
M4Y2J5 B6P6C3 / N3V4A2 P5T7C3,
A9Q5R7 J2X8S7 / M4H6K5 O3P9B2,
T4P2B6 D3G6V3 / S7B3E6 N5F7H1,
M6P4D2 P4B3J5 / Y2D6F1 O7P2H4.

Now John Henry said to his handler
Look yonder at what I see
Your sorter done broke and your mail done choke
And ya can't sort mail like me Lord, Lord
Ya can't sort mail like me.

The letters was flying in the mail room
John Henry was sortin' fire
But he sorted so hard that he broke his poor heart
And he laid down his letters and he died Lord,
And he laid down his letters and he died, Lord, Lord
Laid down his letters and he died.

When the union heard that John Henry
Had drawn his final pay
They put a black band 'round every mail box
And they shut down delivery for the day Lord, Lord
Shut down delivery for the day.

They took John Henry to the Rideau
And buried him in the sand,
And every single postman that comes rollin' by
Says there lies a mail sortin' man Lord, Lord,
There lies a mail sortin' man.

Bob Bossin and Peter Froehlich

When John Henry was a little baby
Sittin' on his daddy's knee
He picked up some letters and he threw them in a pile
He said sortin's gonna to be the death of me Lord, Lord,
Sortin's gonna be the death of me

Well they took John Henry to the mail-room
Just as soon as he could stand
They put him the union gave him three ninety-six an hour
And they said son you're a letter sortin' man Lord, Lord
Son you're a letter sortin' man.

After Dinner Butterflies

They were sitting in the library, drinking coffee.
She noticed that he had a hand in one of his pockets, he seemed to be fiddling with something.

George?

What?

What have you got there?

Nothing, he said.

Show it to me immediately.

It's nothing, he said. He took his hand out of his
pocket and puffed elaborately on his cigar. Good cigar, he said.

No cigar, she said. Take that thing out of your
pocket.

George stood up and leaned against the mantel,
still puffing on his cigar. He pulled a rabbit out of a
vase. Look at the nice rabbit, he said.

Put it away.

He stuck the rabbit out the window and
returned to his chair. He picked up an old
newspaper and started reading it. When he was
sure she wasn't looking he put his hand back into
his pocket.

George!

What.

Let me see it.

There's nothing here.

Oh yes there is. I saw you fiddling with it. Now
let me see it.

All right, he said. He reached into his pocket.
Then he changed his mind. No, you have to guess.

I'm not playing one of your stupid games.

Okay, George said. Let's forget it then. He relit
his cigar and stuck his hand back into his pocket.
Time passed. His cigar went out. Mary got another
cup of coffee. The fire was going. George kept his
hand in his pocket. He got tired of the newspaper.
He went over to the library table and sat down to
work on the jigsaw puzzle. He was so absorbed in a
little bit of orange and green that he didn't hear
Mary sneak up on him.

There, she exclaimed. I've got it. Her hand was
in his pocket. Then she withdrew it, puzzled.
There's nothing there, she said.

They sat back down. A few moments later she
noticed that George was working his hand in his
pocket. When he looked up he saw her watching
him. Do you want to see what's in my pocket?

You don't have anything in your pocket.

Yes I do.

Prove it.

Okay, George said. He reached into his pocket

and pulled out a shiny bit of metal. It appeared to be some sort of complicated miniature. He brought it over to her, holding it cupped in the palm of his hand. But when she reached for it, he drew back. Don't touch, he said. You'll break it. He held it out to her again so she could look at it. It was a metal sphere with little red things sticking out of its silver surface.

What is it? she asked.

It's a spaceship.

That's nice.

Watch this. He walked to the side of the room farthest from the fire. Come here, he said. She stood beside him. He threw his metal gizmo into the fire. There was a clicking sound, metal against brickwork.

Well, she said, you could have done that with a firecracker.

Right, George said. They sat down. After a while Mary noticed that she had, in a very faint way, the same sort of feeling in her stomach that she sometimes got in an elevator.

George, she said.

Yes?

I feel funny. I feel like we're in an elevator.

Or in a spaceship, George said. He walked over to the sideboard and poured himself a glass of sherry. Cheers, he said.

Don't think you can upset me with your silly games.

Oh no, George said.

I was once married to a Hungarian count.

Were there bagpipes at your wedding? Yes there were. I was there. I remember them clearly: they were off key.

Mary crossed her legs and tried to pull her skirt down over her knees. They felt strange, as if something was about to land on them. George, she said, prove to me that we are on a spaceship.

All right, George said. He snapped his fingers. Nothing happened. Then a delicate golden butterfly landed on Mary's right knee. Isn't that beautiful?

Isn't what beautiful? Mary said. She could have sworn that a golden butterfly had landed on her knee.

The music, George said. He turned up the radio so that the library was filled with sounds. A second golden butterfly landed on Mary's knee.

I don't like it, she said. She got up and turned the radio off. The butterflies followed her, circling her head like a halo. Go on, she said when she sat down, flicking at her shoulders, go sit on someone else. But they just came back.

You'd better leave them alone, George said.

Why? I don't like them.

But they like you.

I don't like the feeling of them sitting on my shoulders, watching me.

They're very pretty.

I can't even see them without straining my neck.

I'll get you a mirror, George said.

I don't want a mirror. Let's just forget them and see if they go away.

All right, George said. He lit a new cigar and sipped at his sherry. After a while Mary noticed that he had a hand in his pocket again and seemed to be fiddling with something.

George.

What?

What are you doing now?

Nothing, George said. He took his hand out of his pocket. I'm just trying to get this damned thing turned around.

What thing?

The spaceship.

The butterflies were still perched on Mary's shoulders, waiting patiently. George snapped his fingers again. A white wolf appeared in the middle of the room. Its eyes were as golden as butterflies. It walked over to George's chair, climbed up into it, and licked its paws. Go on, George said. Sit on the floor. The wolf looked up at him and then returned to its paws.

You see? You don't know how to do anything right.

I'm sorry, George said.

What a lovely wolf. Look at its eyes.

I wish it would get off my chair.

It likes you, Mary said. That's why it wants to sit on your chair.

If it really liked me it would get off my chair and fetch a stick or something. He took a cigar from the mantel and waved it in the air. Fetch, doggie, he said. He threw the cigar across the room. The wolf looked at him, looked over at the cigar, raised its eyebrows, and went back to sleep.

That reminds me, Mary said. Did I ever tell you that I was once married to a Hungarian count?

Yes, George said. You just told me five minutes ago. Do you mind if I sit on the arm of your chair? The butterflies were still perched on her shoulders, waiting patiently.

Yes, she said. I do mind. Why don't you stand at the mantel and try to look unconcerned?

There was a knock at the door. Come in, George shouted. A man wearing gray overalls and carrying a toolbox entered the room.

Is this the place with the television?

Yes, George said, it's there in the corner. I don't know what's wrong with it.

Probably blew a tube, the repairman said. It often happens. Nice dog.

Yes.

The repairman pushed the television out from the wall and began poking at its innards.

Do you want a glass of sherry?

No thanks, the man said. He reached into the television and pulled out three stuffed camels. Here's your problem, he said. There were three stuffed camels in the back of your television set.

Oh, George said. I was hiding them there for my wife's birthday.

You should've told me. He turned on the set. Works fine now. He pushed the television back against the wall and packed up his tools. I'll send you a bill, he said, and left the room.

The repairman made two more house calls and then went home. His wife was sitting up, waiting for him. He changed out of his coveralls, washed up, and then got his dinner out of the oven and a beer from the refrigerator.

How did it go tonight?

The usual. Is Jimmy asleep?

Yes, he went to bed hours ago.

What else did you do?

Nothing much, she said. She crossed her legs and tried to pull her skirt down over her knees. I watched TV for a while and read Jimmy a story.

Is there anything for dessert?

There's some pie. He went into the kitchen and found a coconut cream pie in the refrigerator. He brought it back into the living room.

Have you every wanted to throw a piece of pie in my face?

Once, she said. Remember that dance we went to just after we started going out? You put an ice cube down my dress? Well, when you took me home my parents were still up and we had strawberry pie with whipped cream. You were all sitting at the table and I was getting the pie. I could feel the ice water trickling down my skin, and the inside of my dress was wet. I almost dumped the pie right on your head.

He leaned back and lit a cigarette. God, he said, that must have been ten years ago.

Eleven, she said. Eleven years and two months. I remember standing there. I was just about to turn the pie onto your head when I decided to marry you. She crossed the room and sat down beside him on the couch. I don't know why I never told you, she said. I always meant to.

What else didn't you ever tell me?

Did I ever tell you that I was once married to a Hungarian count?

No, he said. And I wouldn't believe you if you did. He was leaning back with his eyes closed. She dipped her hand into the pie and spread it gently over his face. She formed little ridges at the eyebrows, being careful not to get any into his eyes. She spread it on his cheeks with the palms of her hands and then swirled it with her index finger so that his cheeks stood out in spiral puffs. She gave him a moustache and a beard—a nice pointed Vandyke beard that reminded her of a picture. When the beard started to drip she pushed it back up onto his chin and drew a picture of a rose in it. All the whipped cream was gone. She took a fork and fed him some of the coconut filling.

How does it taste?

Good, he said.

I should have saved you some of the whipped cream.

That's all right. He stuck out his tongue and licked a patch along his right cheek. Tonight I saw a woman with two golden butterflies perched on her shoulders.

That's nice, dear.

Matt Cohen

Night Wind

Somewhere out there
we are animals,
in the cold wind always
blowing from death—
breathing its
storm under my
dry skin—
beating bone-music
into the tight black drum
of my fear.

Wind cast us
in all directions—
my face collapsed
in your eyes—
pieces of your heart
came away in my hands.
I felt some strange cold
distance of touch
in your body I've entered
a hundred times.

Wind gives
no reason for taking
only tears at the
blind window
as I lie
silent against you.

Against you.
Our bodies know
what the silence is.

The sound has
no ending like a dream
you never return
to. I still remember
that emptiness—
the first whisper
of darkness and the dead wind rising
all night.

Susan Musgrave

That Yellow Prairie Sky

I was looking at the back of a new dollar bill, at that scene of somewhere on the prairies, and all of a sudden I was looking right through it and I wasn't in Toronto at all anymore—I was back out west. The clouds were moving overhead as if we were traveling and I pointed to that fence that's down and I said, "Look't there, Julie, that must be Tom's place. He hasn't fixed that piece of fence these thirty years." And then I noticed the elevator wasn't getting any closer.

It never does.

My brother Tom, he was quite a guy for women. I'll bet he was the worst for twenty miles on either side of the Battle River. Or the best, whichever way you look at it. I guess I wasn't far behind. Anyway, we spent the winter courting those two girls.

The way it happened, we met them in the fall while we were out hunting. I mean, we knew them all our lives. But you know how it is, eh? You look at some girl all your life, and then one day you stop all of a sudden and take another look and you kind of let out a low whistle.

Well, Tom was twenty-three then, with me a year younger, and we'd grown up together. He taught me how to play hockey and how to snare rabbits and anything new that came along. Out on the prairies you don't have neighbours over your head and in your back yard, and a brother really gets to be a brother.

When it rained that fall and the fields got too soft for threshing we decided to go out and take a crack at some of the ducks that were feeding on our crop. We built a big stook that would keep us out of view, facing the slough hole and the setting sun, and we crawled inside. I can still see it all in my mind . . . .

A thousand and a thousand ducks were milling black against the yellow sky. Like autumn leaves from the tree of life they tumbled in the air; a new flock coming from the north, a flock circling down, a flock tremulous above the water, reluctant to wet a thousand feet. And silhouetted on the far horizon was a threshing machine with a blower pointed at a strawpile, and nearer was the glint of the sun on the slough, and then a rush of wings from behind, overhead, going into the sun, and with a sudden jolt the autumn-sharp smell of a smoking gun.

I let go with both barrels at a flock that was too high up, and before I could reload there was a scream that left my jaw hanging as wide open as the breech of my old twelve-gauge.

"I swear," Tom said, "now ain't that the prettiest pair of mallards that ever came close to losing their pinfeathers?"

I pushed my way out of the stook, and Tom was right.

I guess they didn't see us. I mean, Kay and Julie.

They were standing back of our stook, looking scared, with their skirts tucked into—tucked up—and nobody thought of it in the excitement, or at least they didn't.

"Are you trying to kill us?" Julie asked, pushing back a blond curl and pretending she was only mad and not scared at all.

"Can't you see we're shooting ducks?" Tom said.

"I can't by the number that fell," she said.

That's when I spoke up. "They were too high and I was too anxious."

Julie looked at me and my gun and she blushed. "I didn't mean to insult your shooting. I've heard folks say you're one of the best shots around."

Funny thing. I was pretty good, but just about then I could've told a battalion of the Princess Pat's to back up and drop their guns.

It was then that the redhead, Kay, spoke up. "Really, I'm glad you missed. I hate to see things get killed."

Tom looked up at the distant ducks for a minute, and then said, "As a matter of fact, I hate it myself." It was the first time I ever heard Tom say a thing like that. Most of the time you couldn't hold him.

There was a kind of a loss for words. Then Kay explained, "We're making boxes for the box social in the church hall tonight, and we're taking the short cut over to Rittner's place to borrow four little wheels that the Rittners have left over from the little toy wagon that Halberg's new automobile ran into."

"We're in a terribly hurry," Julie said, "so instead of going around by the road we're going to wade across Rittner's slough—"

And then they noticed it too, and before Tom could say he figured as much, they were in the slough wading above their knees.

"A nice pair of shafts," Tom commented.

"A dandy pair," I said. But I soon found out I was talking about a different pair.

That night at the box social Tom paid three dollars and a half for the lunch box that looked like a pink Red River oxcart with toy wagon wheels on it. He figured it was Kay's because she had red hair, and in a pinch we could make a switch.

Some religious fellow caught on to me and ran

me up to five and a quarter on the yellow one. It was a great help to the church committee, and it looked like a fair enough investment otherwise. Sure enough, I got Kay's and I wanted Julie's, so Tom and I switched and the girls never caught on; or at least they never let on that they did.

Through the rest of the fall and during the winter Dad had to do the chores quite a few times by himself. Tom and I didn't miss a dance or a hayride or a skating party within trotting range of the finest team of dapple grays in the country. We didn't have all the fancy courting facilities that folks here in the east have, but we had lots of space and lots of sky. And we didn't miss much on a frosty night, the old buffalo robe doing whatever was necessary to keep warm . . . .

The northern lights in the winter sky were a silent symphony; flickering white, fading red and green, growing and bursting and dying in swirls and echoes of swirls, in wavering angel-shadows, in shimmering music. And on one edge of the wide white prairie shone a solitary light, and toward it moved a sleigh with the jingle of harness, the clip of hoofs, the squeak of runners on the snow; and the jingling, clopping, squeaking rose up like the horses' frozen breath to the silent music in the sky.

I guess we did pretty well. I remember the night we were driving home from a bean supper and dance, and Julie said, "You're getting pretty free with your behaviour."

"Well, you're going to be my wife soon enough," I said.

"It can't be soon enough," she whispered, and she pushed my arm away. Women are always contrary that way.

Tom and Kay were curled up at the back of the sleigh and they couldn't hear us.

"Let's get out and run behind for a ways," I said. "My feet are getting cold. And I can clap my hands."

"My feet are warm," she said.

"But mine aren't."

"You're just making that up because you're mad."

"Why would I be mad?"

"You're mad because I stopped you."

"Stopped me what?"

She didn't want to say it. "Nothing," she said.

"I think I'll get out and run behind by myself," I said. "Should I?"

She reached up and kissed me right on the mouth, cold and yet warm, and that was that as far as the running behind went.

"Let's talk," she said. "We've only been engaged since midnight, and here you want to act like we're married already."

"Who, me?" I said, trying to sound like I didn't know what she was talking about.

"Let's talk," she said.

"Talk," I said. "I'm all ears."

"Don't you want to talk?"

"Sure I want to talk. If I can get a word in edgewise."

"I can't get used to being engaged," she said. "I want to talk."

"What'll we talk about?" I said. "It seems to me we've done nothing but talk since last fall."

"Let's plan," she said.

That was the end of my plans.

"We're going to get married, remember?" she went on. "You asked me and I said yes before you had hardly asked the second time."

"You weren't so sure I'd ask a third time."

She soon changed that subject. "Kay said that she and Tom are going to build a house this fall."

"It's a good idea. Living on the home place is no good for them and no good for Ma and Dad."

"Why can't we build a house?"

"We got a shack on our place."

"Shack is right. One room and a lean-to."

"It's a roof."

"Kay and Tom are going to get a new bedroom suite and a new stove, and Kay is going to start making new curtains. I could start making new curtains too if we were going to have a new house with lots of windows."

"If we get a good crop, okay. But I got enough stashed away to get married on and put a crop in, and that's it."

"I want to make a nice home for you. We'll have a family."

"We might," I said. "But things'll have to pick up."

"Promise," she said.

"Sure enough," I said.

"I mean promise we'll have a new house."

"Don't you think it would be better to wait and see?"

She didn't answer.

"We might flood out or dry out or freeze out. How do I know?"

She still didn't answer.

"What if it's a grasshopper year? What about wireworms and wild oats and rust and buckwheat?"

"Promise me," she said. "I don't even think you love me."

That was her final word.

I talked for another ten minutes about wireworms and rust, and after that things got quiet. We sat in that sleigh for an hour, our breath freezing in our scarves (twenty-seven below, it was), wrapped in a buffalo robe and in each other's arms and never once did she speak. To a young fellow twenty-two years old it didn't make much sense. But I didn't push her away. She was soft and warm and quiet; and I thought she had fallen asleep.

"Okay," I said, finally. "Okay okay okay. I promise."

She snuggled closer.

We had a double wedding in the spring.

Tom's father-in-law fixed up two granaries near the house and we held the reception at his place. Everybody was there. My cousin had trouble with the pump, and while everybody was watching him trying to tap the keg, Tom came over to where I was watching the sky for a nice day and he shook my hand.

"We're the luckiest pair of duck hunters this side of the fourth meridian," he said. "We've each got a half section that's almost paid for, we've got a big crop to put in that'll put us on our feet, and we've each got the prettiest girl in the country. How do you like being a married man?"

"Yes, sir," I said. I had one eye on a couple of my old sidekicks who were kissing the bride for the second time. "This here love business is the clear McCoy."

I remember that my cousin drew the first pitcherful just then, and it was all foam. But we were only just married . . . .

The sky was the garment of love. It was a big sky, freckled with the stars of the universe; a happy sky, shrouding all the pain. It was the time of spring, and spring is love, and in the night sky arrow after arrow of honking geese winged across the yellow moon, driving winter from the world.

Right after the wedding we moved into the shack and really went to work. I was busy from morning till night putting in a big crop, while Julie helped with the chores and looked after her little chicks and put in a big garden. When the crop was in we started on the summer fallow, and before that was done it was haying time.

At noon she brought dinner out to me in the field, out in the sun and the wind, and we sat side by side and talked and laughed, and the dust from my face got on hers sometimes, and sometimes I didn't get started quite on time. And the weather was good too . . . .

In the evening a black cloud towered up in the west and tumbled over the land, bringing lightning and rain and hope. In the morning there was only a fragment of cloud; the dot worn on a woman's cheek beside a pair of beautiful eyes, and the beautiful sun in the fair blue sky sent warmth and growth into the earth, and the rain and the sun turned the black fields green, the green fields yellow.

I remember one Sunday we went over to Tom's for a chicken supper. Tom and Dad and I talked about the way the crops were coming along and where to get binder repairs, and we made arrangements to help each other with the cutting and stooking.

The womenfolk talked about their gardens and their chickens until Julie mentioned the drapes she was sewing.

"I'm going to have one of those living room parlours," she said, "one of those living room parlours with lots of windows, like in the magazines, and I'm making drapes for that kind of window."

"I think I will too," Kay said. "Tom cut some of the nicest plans out of last week's *Free Press*. I hope the fall stays nice."

"My husband is even getting enthusiastic," Julie said, giving me a teasing smile. "I caught him holding up the drapes one day and looking at them."

Ma said she was crocheting some new pillow covers for all the plllows and easy chairs that seemed to be coming up, and she thought they all better get together and do some extra canning. Entertaining takes food.

Kay said, "Ma," meaning her mother-in-law, "you'll soon have your house all to yourself again. And since Tom is afraid he'll have to help with the washing, he's going to get me a new washing machine."

"We might pick up a secondhand car," Julie said, "if the crop on our breaking doesn't go down because it's too heavy."

I had mentioned it'd be something to tinker on during the winter.

It wasn't long before Julie was talking about the washing machine and Kay was talking about a secondhand car. Wheat was a good price that year.

We menfolk laughed at the women and we found a few things in the Eaton's catalogue that we could use ourselves. It seemed that somebody was always coming up with something new that we couldn't possibly do without.

After supper we all walked out to have a look at Tom's crop. Tom could even make a gumbo patch grow wheat.

I guess it happened a week later. I mean, the

storm. Julie was working on her drapes. It was a hot day, too hot and too still, and in the afternoon the clouds began to pile up in the west . . . .

The storm came like a cloud of white dust high in the sky; not black or gray like a rain cloud, but white; and now it was rolling across the heavens with a brute unconcern for the mites below, and after a while came the first dull roar. The hot, dead air was suddenly cool, stirring to a breeze, and then a white wall of destruction bridged earth and sky and moved across the land and crashed across the fields of ripening grain.

Old man Rittner saw it coming west of us, and he went out and drove his ax in the middle of the yard, figuring to split her. But she didn't split.

In fifteen minutes it was all over and the sun was shining as pretty as you please. Only there was no reason for the sun to shine. Our garden and our fields were flat, and the west window was broken, and half the shingles were gone from the shack. The leaves were half stripped from the trees, and the ground was more white than black and, I remember, the cat found a dead robin.

My wife didn't say a word.

I hitched up old Mag to the buggy and Julie and I drove over to Tom's place.

Tom was sitting on the porch steps with his head in his hands, and Kay was leaning on the fence, looking at her garden. It looked like they hadn't been talking much either.

I got out and walked over to Tom, and Julie stayed in the buggy.

"A hundred percent," I said.

"The works," he said. "And all I got is enough insurance to feed us this winter or to buy a ticket to hell out of here."

"The same with me," I said.

We couldn't think of much to say.

All of a sudden Tom almost shouted at Kay: "Say it and get it over with. If you want we'll go to the city and I'll get a job. I can get on a construction gang. They're paying good now. We'll get a washing machine and a secondhand car." He looked at his wheat fields, beaten flat. "We'll make a payment and get our own house."

He kicked at a hailstone.

"A house with big windows for my new drapes," Kay added.

Tom got up and he walked to the gate where Julie sat in the buggy. Kay and I, we stood there watching him, almost afraid of the storm in his eyes, and Kay looked at me as if I should stop him before he went and grabbed a pitchfork or something.

"Tom, I was joking," Kay said. "I don't need fancy curtains and a washing machine. And we never needed a car before. Did we, Tom? We got enough for us and Ma and Dad. Haven't we, Tom? And we got next year."

Tom snorted at that idea. He kicked open the gate and walked out toward the barn. There was so much helpless anger in him he couldn't talk.

Kay called after him. "We still got this, Tom." She was kind of crying. She was pointing at the black dirt that showed through the broken grass. "Look, Tom, we still got this."

Tom, he stopped in the middle of the yard and he turned around. For a long time he was only looking at Kay's empty hand.

All of a sudden he bent down like he was going to say a prayer or something. And he scooped up a handful of hailstones, and he flung them back at the sky.

Like I say, my wife; she didn't say a word.

Robert Kroetsch

The Dream

I open the door from the bathroom
to the corridor. A small
blond child is standing there.
He looks at me.
"Who are you?" I ask. He says, "God."

Tom Marshall

The Wind, God and the Prairie

Here was the least common denominator of nature, the skeleton requirements simply, of land and sky—Saskatchewan prairie. It lay wide around the town, stretching tan to the far line of the sky, shimmering under the June sun and waiting for the unfailing visitation of wind, gentle at first, barely stroking the long grasses and giving them life; later, a long hot gusting that would lift the black topsoil and pile it in barrow pits along the roads, or in deep banks against the fences.

Over the prairie, cattle stood listless beside the dried-up slough beds which held no water for them. Where the snow-white of alkali edged the course of the river, a thin trickle of water made its way toward the town low upon the horizon. Silver willow, heavy with dust, grew along the riverbanks, perfuming the air with its honey smell.

Just before the town the river took a wide loop and entered at the eastern edge. Inhabited now by some eighteen hundred souls, it had grown up on either side of the river from the seed of one homesteader's sod hut built in the spring of eighteen seventy-five. It was made up largely of frame buildings with high, peaked roofs, each with an expanse of lawn in front and a garden in the back; they lined avenues with prairie names: Bison, Riel, Qu'Appelle, Blackfoot, Fort. Cement sidewalks extended from First Street to Sixth Street at MacTaggart's Corner; from that point to the prairie a boardwalk ran.

Lawn sprinklers sparkled in the sun; Russian poplars stood along either side of Sixth Street. Five houses up from MacTaggart's Corner stood the O'Connal home, a three-storied house lifting high above the white cottage to the left of it. Virginia creepers had almost smothered the veranda; honeysuckle and spirea grew on either side of the steps. A tricycle with its front wheel sharply turned stood in the middle of the walk.

The tricycle belonged to Brian Sean MacMurray O'Connal, the four-year-old son of Gerald O'Connal, druggist, and Maggie O'Connal, formerly Maggie MacMurray of Trossachs, Ontario. Brian at the moment was in the breakfast room. He sat under the table at the window, imagining himself an ant deep in a dark cave. Ants, he had decided, saw things tiny and grass-colored, and his father and mother would never know about it. He hated his mother and his father and his grandmother for spending so much time with the baby, for making it a blanket tent and none for

him. Not that he cared; he needed no one to play with him now that he was an ant. He was a smart ant.

He hadn't asked Dr. Svarich, with his bitter smell, to play with him. He would never again ask anyone to play with him. He would make them wish they had never been mean to him.

"Brian!"

His grandmother stood high above him. Looking up to her he could see her face turned down, could see the dark velvet band circling high around her throat, hooping in the twin folds of skin that hung from under her chin. Light stabbed out from her silver-rimmed glasses.

"I told ye to go outside!"

He crawled from under the table and stood by her hand with large liver spots spattering its back, and blue veins writhing under the thin skin. Her hand had great knotted knuckles. When her stomach sang after dinner, Brian promised himself, he would not listen.

"I will not speak to ye again!" The loose folds of her cheeks shook slightly as she spoke. The winy bouquet of tonic was about her, reminding him of apples. Behind the spectacles her eyes looked forbidding to him. "If ye stay inside ye'll disturb the baby. Ye must go out!"

"Can I have a tent like the baby has?"

"Ye cannot. 'Tis bad enough having the baby ill without—"

"Is he ill bad?"

"Aye," said his grandmother. "Now, be a good boy and do as ye're told."

He would get Jake Harris, the town policeman, after her. He hoped Jake would bring his policeman's knife and chop her into little pieces and cut her head off, for making him go outside to play.

He stood on the step of the back porch a moment, feeling the warmth of the sun against his cheek, the wind, which was beginning to rise now that it was late afternoon, delicately active about his ears and at his nostrils.

Slowly he walked to the sand pile by the high Caragana hedge that separated the O'Connal back yard from that of Sherry next door. He hated his grandmother. She made him go out to a sand pile where there was nobody but an old shovel to play with. Reflectively he stared down at the sand hump in one corner of the box. It was like an ant pile, he thought; perhaps if he waited an ant might come out. He watched impatiently, and then as no ant emerged, he took up the shovel that lay at his feet. He hit the bump, and wished that it were his grandmother. He hit the bump again, being careful that it was with the sharp edge and not the flat bottom of the shovel. He was hitting his grandmother so awful she was bawling her head off.

He stopped.

Directly opposite him, and low in the hedge, was a round and freckled face—a new face to Brian. He began again to punish the sand pile.

The boy came to the edge of the sand pile. Hedge leaves hung to his sweater and to his hat, a blue sailor hat bearing the legend HMS THUNDERBOLT. It had got twisted so that the ribbon hung down his snub nose.

"I'm coming into the sand pile." As he stepped over, Brian saw that his knees were scratched, that his hands were fat with deep crease-lines at the wrists, like the baby's. "Let me hit some," the boy said.

"No," Brian said.

"I'm Benny Banana."

"Benny Banana—Benny Banana," chanted Brian; "Banana-Benny-Banana."

The boy sat down; he picked up a thin pebble from the sand. "What's your name?"

Brian plumped himself down by the boy. "Brian Sean MacMurray O'Connal," he said.

"I'm Forbsie Hoffman." The boy touched the tip of his tongue with the pebble he had picked up. The pebble hung. To Brian it was magic.

"I'm going to do that. I'm going to hang to my tongue." He tried it. "Mine won't hang at all."

"Naw 'hinny enouch," said Forbsie, with the pebble still clinging to the tip of his protruding tongue.

Brian found that a skinnier pebble hung.

Forbsie said, "*Thpt*."

Brian said, "*Thpt*."

"Do you know anything more?" asked Brian.

"I'm hungry. Maybe if you was to ask, your maw'd give us a piece."

"The baby's going to heaven," explained Brian.

"My Dad's a conductor," Forbsie said, "on the CPR. He has got silver buttons."

"It's where God stays," said Brian, "heaven."

"No it ain't," said Forbsie. He lifted his arm and pointed. "God lives right in town. Over there. I seen Him lots of times."

"Where?"

"At His house."

"You have not!"

"Oh, yes! He's all grapes and bloody. He carries around a lamb."

Brian got up. "Let's us go over to His place."

Forbsie got up. "I guess I'll go home. I don't feel so much like going."

"I've got something to say to Him. I'm going to get Him after my gramma. You show me where He lives."

"All right," said Forbsie.

The wind had strengthened; it had begun to snap the clothes on Sherry's line, where Mrs. Sherry, a tall, spare woman, was in the act of hanging up her washing. She took a clothespin from her mouth. "How is the baby today, Brian?"

"He's very sick," Brian told her. "This is Forbsie. We're going to see Someone."

Mrs. Sherry, with limp underwear in her hands, stared after the boys as they walked toward the front of the house.

At MacTaggart's Corner a tall man in shirt sleeves greeted them: Mr. Digby, Principal of the school. He walked a block west with them from the corner. Digby could not be called a handsome man, largely because of the angularity of his face. His skin had the weathered look of split rock that has lain long under sun and wind. His sandy eyebrows were unruly over eyes of startling blueness; his hair lay in one fair shock over his forehead.

"We're going to see Somebody," Brian told him.

"Are you," said Digby.

"Yes," said Brian: "God."

The schoolmaster showed no surprise. "I'd like to come with you, but I have a previous engagement."

"What's that?" asked Brian.

"It means that I can't go," said Digby.

When the boys had turned off Bison Avenue and left the Principal, they walked in silence over the cement sidewalk. Once they bent down to watch a bee crawl over a Canadian thistle, his licorice all-sorts stripes showing through the cellophane of folded wings. Down the road, from time to time, a dust-devil spun—snatching up papers, dust, and debris, lifting them up, carrying them high into the air, and leaving them finally to sink slowly down again.

"Step on a crack," Forbsie sang, "break your mother's back!"

Brian sang, "Step on a crack, break my gramma's back!" He did not miss stepping upon a single crack in the three blocks that took them to the great, gray, sandstone church: KNOX PRESBYTERIAN—1902.

"Is this it?" asked Brian.

Forbsie said that it was.

"Let's go see Him, then."

"I'm going home, I think. It's suppertime, and I better get home."

"Not yet." Brian started up the stone steps; when he turned at the top, he saw that Forbsie was halfway down the block, his head turned back over his shoulder. Brian knocked on the church door. As he did, he felt the wind ruffling his hair. Forbsie was down by the corner now.

A woman came out of the little brown house next to the church. She shook a mop, then turned to re-enter the house. She stopped as she saw Brian; stood watching him. A fervent whirlwind passed the brown house with the woman standing on the porch; at the trees before the church, it rose suddenly, setting every leaf in violent motion, as though an invisible hand had gripped the trunks and shaken them.

Brian wondered why Forbsie had not wanted to come. He knocked again. It was simply that God was in the bathroom and couldn't come right away.

As he turned away from the door, he saw the woman staring at him. She ought to know if God was in. He went down the steps and to the opening in the hedge.

"I guess God isn't anywhere around."

"Why—what do you mean?"

"That's His house, isn't it?"

"Yes."

"I'm going to see Him."

The woman stared at him silently a moment; under the slightly gray hair pulled severely back, her face wore an intense look. "God isn't—He isn't the same as other people, you know. He's a spirit."

"What's that?"

"It's someone—something you can't hear—or see, or touch." Her gray eyes were steady upon his face; he noted that her teeth had pushed back her upper lip slightly, giving her a permanent smile.

"Does He smell?"

"No, he doesn't. I think you better talk with my husband. He's the minister and he could tell you much more about this than I could," she said, with relief loosening the words.

"Does he know God pretty well?"

"Pretty well. He—he tells people about Him."

"Better than you do? Does he know better than you do?"

"It's—it's his job to know God."

"My dad is a druggist. He works for God, I guess."

"He works for God," the woman agreed.

"My Uncle Sean isn't a sheepherder—neither is Ab. Ab's got a thing on his foot, and one foot is shorter, so he goes up and down when he walks."

"And who is Ab?" the woman asked him.

"Uncle Sean's hired man that feeds the pigs and helps grow the wheat whenever there isn't any goddam-drought."

The woman looked startled.

"Has your husband got calfs?" Brian asked her.

"No—he hasn't any calfs—calves." She looked quickly back over her shoulder.

"He looks after the sheeps and the sheep pups."

"Looks after the . . . !"

"I'm going to get God after my gramma," Brian confided. "She has a thing on her leg too. It is not the same as Ab's. You only see it on the heel. She's got room-a-ticks in a leg."

The woman cast another anxious look over her shoulder.

"She belshes," said Brian, "a lot."

"Perhaps your grandmother has stomach trouble."

"If your husband works for God, then he could take me in His house for a while, couldn't he?"

"Perhaps he could. Tomorrow."

"Not now?"

"Tomorrow—in the morning—after breakfast." She turned to the doorway.

"Does God like to be all grapes and bloody?"

"All what?"

"That's what I want to see."

"But what do you mean . . . ?"

"Something's burning," said Brian. "I'll come back."

She hurried in to her burning dinner.

Brian walked back towards his home. He did not turn down Bison Avenue where it crossed the street upon which the church was, but continued on, a dark wishbone of a child wrapped in reflection.

The wind was persistent now, a steady urgency upon his straight back, smoking up the dust from the road along the walk, lifting it and carrying it out to the prairie beyond. Several times Brian stopped; once to look up into the sun's unbearable radiance and then away with the lingering glow stubborn in his eyes; another time when he came upon a fox-red caterpillar making a procession of itself over a crack that snaked along the walk. He squashed it with his foot. Further on he paused as a spider that carried its bead of a body between hurrying thread-legs. Death came for the spider too.

He looked up to find that the street had stopped. Ahead lay the sudden emptiness of the prairie. For the first time in his four years of life he was alone on the prairie.

He had seen it often, from the veranda of his uncle's farmhouse, or at the end of a long street,

but till now he had never heard it. The hum of telephone wires along the road, the ring of hidden crickets, the stitching sound of grasshoppers, the sudden relief of a meadow lark's song, were deliciously strange to him. Without hesitation he crossed the road and walked out through the hip-deep grass stirring in the steady wind; the grass clung at his legs; haloed fox-tails bowed before him; grasshoppers sprang from hidden places in the grass, clicketing ahead of him to disappear, then lift again.

A gopher squeaked questioningly as Brian sat down upon a rock warm to the backs of his thighs. He picked a pale blue flax-flower at his feet, stared long at the stripings in its shallow throat, then looked up to see a dragonfly hanging on shimmering wings directly in front of him. The gopher squeaked again, and he saw it a few yards away, sitting up, watching him from its pulpit hole. A suave-winged hawk chose that moment to slip its shadow over the face of the prairie.

And all about him was the wind now, a pervasive sighing through great emptiness, unhampered by the buildings of the town, warm and living against his face and in his hair.

Then for the second time that day he saw a strange boy—one who came from behind him soundlessly, who stood and stared at him with steady gray eyes in a face of remarkable broadness, with cheekbones circling high under a dark and freckled skin. He saw that the boy's hair, bleached as the dead prairie grass itself, lay across his forehead in an all-round cowlick curling under at the edge. His faded blue pants hung open in two tears just below the knees. He was barefooted.

Brian was not startled; he simply accepted the boy's presence out here as he had accepted that of the gopher and the hawk and the dragonfly.

"This is your prairie," Brian said.

The boy did not answer him. He turned and walked as silently as he had come, out over the prairie. His walk was smooth.

After the boy's figure had become just a speck in the distance, Brian looked up into the sky, now filled with a soft expanse of cloud, the higher edges luminous and startling against the blue. It stretched to the prairie's rim. As he stared, the gray underside carded out, and through the cloud's softness was revealed a blue well shot with sunlight. Almost as soon as it had cleared, a whisking of cloud stole over it.

For one moment no wind stirred. A butterfly went pelting past. God, Brian decided, must like the boy's prairie.

W.O. Mitchell, from the novel *Who Has Seen the Wind*

Acknowledgements

We are grateful to the following for permission to reprint the copyright materials. While we have made every effort to locate authors and publishers, we welcome notice of any errors and omissions and will make certain to correct them in future editions.

"A sort of dedication" by Victoria Swettenham and Peter Carver.

"I, Icarus", from *Bread, Wine and Salt* by Alden Nowlan, copyright ©1961 by Clarke, Irwin & Company Ltd.

"Mati Laansoo Tests the Law of Gravity", by permission of Mati Laansoo, reprinted from *Peter Gzowski's Book About This Country in the Morning,* 1974, Hurtig Publishers.

"Rescue Flight", excerpt from *Bush Pilot With a Briefcase,* by Ronald A. Keith, 1972, Doubleday Canada Ltd.

"Incredible Achievement!! Canadian War Ace Downs Five Enemy Planes!!!" and "Billy Bishop - Solo Air Duellist", excerpts from *Canada's Fighting Pilots* by Edmund Cosgrove, Clarke, Irwin & Company Ltd.

"The End of the Red Baron", from *Knights of the Air* by John Norman Harris, reprinted by permission of the Macmillan Company of Canada Ltd.

"Flying/Spring of '44", by permission of Mary Lynn Hammond.

"Flying a Red Kite" by Hugh Hood from *Flying a Red Kite,* Ryerson Press, reprinted by permission of Oberon Press.

"It's in the Egg, in the Little Round Egg", from *Top Soil* by Joe Rosenblatt, by permission of Press Porcepic Ltd.

"The Black Fly Song" by Wade Hemsworth, by permission of Southern Music Ltd.

"Lark Song" by W.P. Kinsella, reprinted from *Dance Me Outside,* by permission of Oberon Press.

"Mouth Organ Symphony" and "The King and That Woman", excerpts from *Ten Lost Years* by Barry Broadfoot, Doubleday Canada Ltd.

"Music", by permission of David Bittle.

"Flowers for Lightfoot", by permission of Dave Cavanagh.

"The Price of Progress", excerpt from *The Canadian Inventions Book* by Janis Nostbakken and Jack Humphrey, Greey de Pencier Books.

"The Broadcaster's Poem" and "A Note on the Public Transportation System", from *I'm a Stranger Here Myself* by Alden Nowlan, copyright © 1974 by Clarke, Irwin & Company Ltd.

"The Perils of Max", excerpt from *And Now Here's Max* by Max Ferguson, copyright © 1967 by McGraw-Hill Ryerson Ltd.

"Family Snapshots", by permission of Richard Hornsey.

"This is a Photograph of Me" by Margaret Atwood, by permission of House of Anansi.

"Me as My Grandmother", from *Two Kinds of Honey* by Rosemary Aubert, reprinted by permission of Oberon Press.

"Ham on Wheels", by permission of Andreas Schroeder, reprinted from *Weekend.*

"Tee Vee Man", from *North by 2000* by H.A. Hargreaves, Peter Martin Associates Ltd.

"Violence, Envy, Rage", by permission of Robert Fulford.

"Ontario Secondary School Students Discuss 1867 in 1967", from *Translations from the English* by J.R. Colombo, Peter Martin Associates Ltd.

"Next to Nothing At All", from *You May Know Them as Sea Urchins, Ma'am* by Ray Guy, edited by Eric Norman, Breakwater Books Ltd.

"Political Speech" and "Youth and Bliss", from *As It Happened* by Barbara Frum, reprinted by permission of McClelland and Stewart Ltd. Toronto.

"Hat" by Joe Hall, by permission of Eyeball Wine Music, CAPAC.

"Everybody Knows But Me" by Jesse Winchester, copyright © 1976 Fourth Floor Music Inc. & Hot Kitchen Music. All Rights Reserved. Used by Permission.

"Women" by Claire Martin, translated by Philip Stratford, from *Voices from Quebec,* copyright © 1977 by Van Nostrand Reinhold Ltd. Toronto, reprinted by permission of Van Nostrand Reinhold Ltd. and of Le Cercle du Livre de France.

"Housewife", by permission of Helen Porter.

"On the Road to LaScie", "Shanadithit", and "Consomme and Coca Cola", by permission of Al Pittman and Breakwater Books Ltd.

"Dancing", from *The Dance Is One* by F.R. Scott, McClelland and Stewart Ltd. By permission of the author.

"Dancer With Bruised Knees" by Anna McGarrigle, copyright ©1977 by Anna McGarrigle, administered by Garden Court Music, ASCAP. All rights reserved.

"Poet Cop" by Martin O'Malley, by permission of *The Globe and Mail.*

"Tracks", from *Poet Cop* by Hans Jewinski, PaperJacks Ltd.

"Do the Panthers Play the Blues for Stephanie", by permission of Hans Jewinski.

"The Natural Thing", by permission of bp Nichol.

"Jacques Cartier" by Robert Charlebois, translated by Philip Stratford, from *Voices from Quebec* , copyright ©1977 by Van Nostrand Reinhold Ltd. Reprinted by permission.

"Hanging Loose in the Heavens" by Joann Webb, by permission of *Weekend.*

"Cool Wind from the North" by Sylvia Fricker Tyson, copyright © Newtonville Music Inc., by permission of Chappell & Company Ltd. Toronto.

"The Stranger Song" by Leonard Cohen, copyright ©1967 by Project Seven Music, division of CTMP Inc. New York.

"Hey That's No Way to Say Goodbye" by Leonard Cohen, copyright ©1967 Stranger Music Inc. All rights reserved.

"Downtown Streets", "Quiet", and "Ending", by permission of Miriam Waddington, from *The Price of Gold* by Miriam Waddington, 1976, Oxford University Press.

"When I Was a Little Girl", from *A Choice of Dreams* by Joy Kogawa, reprinted by permission of McClelland and Stewart Ltd. Toronto.

"Maiden Aunt", by permission of Anne Corkett.

"Forerunners", from *Bluenose Ghosts* by Helen Creighton, copyright © and reprinted by permission of McGraw-Hill Ryerson Ltd.

"Lines for Ohiyesa, the Sioux", by permission of Gail Fox.

"The Witch Canoe", from *The Magic Fiddler* by Claude Aubry, Peter Martin Associates Ltd.

"A Message from the Management", from *Colombo's Little Book of Canadian Proverbs, Graffiti, Limericks and Other Vital Matters,* by permission of J.R. Colombo.

"Plastic Grass, Aluminum Seats . . . Debased Ball?" by Bob Bossin, from The Mermaid Inn, *The Globe and Mail,* by permission of Bob Bossin.

"The Olympic Dream Game" by R. (Jumbles) Scott and J. (Duck) Mock, as recorded by the Pear of Pied Pumkin © 1976 Gahndavara Music (PRO) Canada.

"Mail-Sortin' Man", by permission of Bob Bossin.

"After Dinner Butterflies", by permission of Matt Cohen.

"Night Wind", from *The Impstone* by Susan Musgrave, reprinted by permission of McClelland and Stewart Ltd. Toronto.

"That Yellow Prairie Sky" by Robert Kroetsch, from *Creation,* by permission of New Press, Don Mills, Ontario.

"The Dream", from *The Earth-Book* by Tom Marshall, reprinted by permission of Oberon Press.

"The Wind, God and Prairie", excerpt from *Who Has Seen the Wind* by W.O. Mitchell, reprinted by permission of the Macmillan Company of Canada Ltd.

Quotations throughout the text courtesy of John Robert Colombo, from *Colombo's Canadian Quotations,* Hurtig Publishers, and *Colombo's Little Book of Canadian Proverbs, Graffiti, Limericks and Other Vital Matters,* Hurtig Publishers.

Art Direction and design T. Wynne-Jones
Cover by Jerrard
Music Copyist Doug Jamieson

Illustration credits

Tim Wynne-Jones 6, 100
Jerrard 8, 76
Leoung O'Young 12, 32, 53, 116
Ken Steacy 14, 16, 18, 19, 20, 21, 59
Rob Macintyre 29, 89, 112
Willy Ashworth 35, 65, 79
Tony Jenkins 37, 45, 85
Karen Fletcher 48
Dale Cummings 63, 75
Peter McLay 93
Diana McElroy 96, 97
M. Hathaway 103

Photo credits

Birgitte Nielsen 1, 2, 3
Leighton McLeod 71, 72
Ted Kawano 46, 47, 86, 87, 106, 107, 117
AP. Wirephoto 80, 81
Randall Hill *The Albertan* 82

Canadian Cataloguing in Publication Data

Main entry under title:

Air

(Elements)

ISBN 0-88778-163-2

1. Readers – 1950-   I. Carver, Peter, 1936-
II. Series.

PE1121.A37   428'.6   C77-001596-4

PETER MARTIN ASSOCIATES LIMITED
280 Bloor Street West, Toronto, Ontario M5S 1W1